HEATH SCIENCE

HEATH SCIENCE

Authors **James P. Barufaldi**
Professor of Science Education
University of Texas, Austin

George T. Ladd
Professor of Education
Boston College

Alice Johnson Moses
Elementary Science Teacher
University of Chicago Laboratory School

Consulting Authors **Herman and Nina Schneider**

Content Consultants Stephen S. Barshay
Assistant Professor of Chemistry
Rhode Island College
Providence, Rhode Island

Joan G. Creager
Professor of Science
Marymount College of Virginia
Arlington, Virginia

John A. Day
Professor of Physics and Meteorology Emeritus
Linfield College
McMinnville, Oregon

Victor J. Mayer
Professor of Science Education and Geology
Ohio State University
Columbus, Ohio

R. Robert Robbins
Piper Professor of Astronomy
University of Texas
Austin, Texas

Frederick J. Stare, M.D.
Professor of Nutrition Emeritus
Harvard University School of Public Health
Boston, Massachusetts

J. Kenneth Taylor
Chairman of the Biology Department
Westfield State College
Westfield, Massachusetts

Jearl Walker
Professor of Physics
Cleveland State University
Cleveland, Ohio

D.C. Heath and Company
Lexington, Massachusetts   Toronto

Project Editor: Paul P. Scopa

Assistant Editor: Roland E. Boucher

Book Designer: Eleanor Thayer

Production Coordinator: Donna Lee Porter

Reading Level Consultants: J & F
Milton Jacobson, *Founder*
Charlottesville, Virginia

Testing and Evaluation Consultant: Peter W. Airasian
Professor, Educational Testing and Evaluation
Boston College, Chestnut Hill, Massachusetts

Educational Consultants

Sister Marie Andre Guay, RSM
Catholic School Office
Providence, Rhode Island

Elaine S. Barrett
Science Project Teacher
Bellevue School District, Washington

Harriett Brookman
Elementary Teacher
Miami, Florida

Napoleon Bryant, Jr.
Professor of Education
Xavier University, Cincinnati, Ohio

Jerry Hayes
Elementary Science Supervisor
Chicago, Illinois

David Lawrence
District Chairperson Science
Hartford, Connecticut

Richard Merrill
Curriculum Specialist
Mt. Diablo Unified School District, Concord, California

Constance Tate
Coordinator, Office of Science
Baltimore, Maryland

Roger Van Bever
Supervisor of Elementary Science
Detroit, Michigan

Mary Ellen Wandel
Supervisory Instructional Specialist
Pittsburgh, Pennsylvania

Edwin P. White
School of Education
University of South Carolina, Spartanburg

Field Test Teachers

Grateful acknowledgment is given to the teachers and students who participated in field tests of Heath Science.

Phoenix, ARIZONA
Lookout Mountain School, Barbara Semmens
Acacia School, Rebecca Walker

Louisville, COLORADO
Louisville Elementary School, Dorothy Pecina, Cheryl Turvey

Boulder, COLORADO
Bear Creek Elementary School, Barbara Puzio, Beverly Vance, Virginia Holland

Merritt Island, FLORIDA
Audubon Elementary School, Sue Colley, Natalie Jerkins, Peggy Graham, Ann Ehren

Satellite Beach, FLORIDA
Surfside Elementary School, Crystal Otto, Judith Cordrey, Sue Wisler

Atlanta, GEORGIA
E. Rivers School, Lillie Thompson, Virginia Robb, Cecelia J. Thomas, Sandra L. Black

Lexington, MASSACHUSETTS
Bowman Elementary School, Maureen Sullivan
Maria Hastings School, Alice F. Baylies

Maynard, MASSACHUSETTS
Coolidge School, Ellen Holway, Elizabeth Niland
Green Meadow School, Daria Benham, Pamela Tiramani

Newton, MASSACHUSETTS
Oak Hill School, Francis R. Stec, Dorothy Mims

Brooklyn, NEW YORK
Blessed Sacrament School, Marilyn Robinson
St. Jerome School, Sr. Patricia Brennan, R.S.M.

Plainview, NEW YORK
Parkway School, Edna Publicker, Shirley Grant
Pasadena School, Muriel Phillips, Suzanne Freund

Norfolk, VIRGINIA
Mary Calcott Elementary School, Barbara Wright
Ocean Air School, Yolanda Hill
Engleside School, Naomi Bethea
Poplar Halls School, Christine Crouch

Cover and Frontispiece Photo: Stacked Logs by Werner H. Müller, Peter Arnold Inc.
Photo illustration credits appear on page 345.

TABLE OF CONTENTS

Unit I   Structures of Insect Life   1
          Chapter 1   The Insect World   3

Unit II   Structures Make Work Easier   41
          Chapter 2   Machines and Force   43
          Chapter 3   Bones and Muscles   79

Unit III Structures Explain the Behavior of Matter   109
          Chapter 4   Matter   111
          Chapter 5   The Earth's Atmosphere   141

Unit IV   Structures Describe the Solar System   179
          Chapter 6   The Solar System   181
          Chapter 7   Traveling Through the Solar
                      System   207

Unit V   Structures of Our Planet's Resources   243
          Chapter 8   The Earth's Rocks   245
          Chapter 9   Sunlight and Green Plants   275
          Chapter 10 The Earth's Resources   299

Unit 1

Structures of Insect Life

The Insect World

You can find insects almost anywhere in the world. Turn over a rock or poke around an old log. Look under plant leaves, in the feathers of birds, and in the fur of cats. You can find insects on an orange peel, inside books, and even on your clothing.

In the city or in the country, in hot or in cold places, you can find insects.

Why do you find insects in so many places? Because there are so many different kinds of insects. Each kind of insect has its own way of fitting into the place where it lives.

photo at left: Studying insects

How Insects Are Alike

If there are so many kinds of insects, all so different, why are they all called insects?

Count the number of legs on each of these insects. Adult insects always have six legs that are jointed.

Weevil

Checkered beetle

Walking stick

Earwig

Aedes mosquito

Housefly

Adult insects are alike in another way. Whether they are fat, flat, long, or short, their bodies have three parts. All insects have a **head,** a **thorax** [THOHR-aks], and an **abdomen** [AB-duh-muhn]. On some insects it is hard to see three separate parts, but they are there.

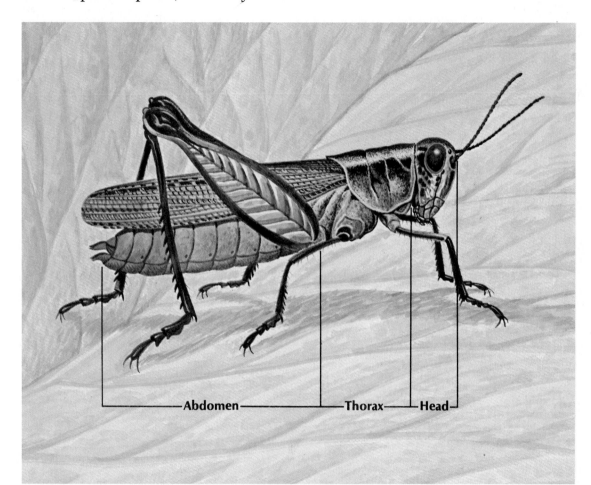

Abdomen————————Thorax——Head

Find the three body parts of the grasshopper in the picture. Find the body parts of a real grasshopper, if you have one. What are the body parts of the other insects that you see pictured?

Insects are alike in still another way. They have outside **skeletons** [SKEHL-uh-tuhnz]. That is, the outside of their bodies is hard. Their outside skeletons hold them up and give them their shapes. Where is your skeleton?

Cricket

Earwig

Rhinoceros beetle

Scarab beetle

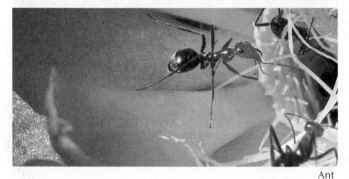
Ant

Wasp

Flower fly

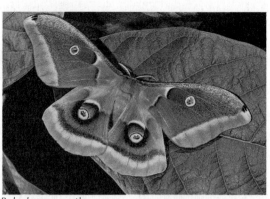

Polyphemus moth

Harvester ants

Crane fly

Dragonfly

Silverfish

An outside skeleton, three body parts, and six legs—these are things all adult insects have. Many insects also have wings. In the pictures, which insects have two pairs of wings? Which have one pair? Which have no wings?

You can find out how insects are alike by finding some insects yourself. You will need an old sheet, a large jar, and some damp sand or soil. Also get some twigs and leaves, a cloth cover for the jar, a rubber band, and a hand lens.

Put some damp soil or sand in the jar. Now place some twigs and leaves on the soil or sand.

Spread a sheet under a bush. You will find bushes even in city parks or a back yard. Shake the bush a few times. You should then find some insects on the sheet. Pick up the corners of the sheet and shake the insects into the middle. Now trap the insects in your jar. Cover the jar with the cloth and hold it in place with the rubber band.

With your hand lens, look at the insects you have found. You can keep them in the jar while you look at them. Try to answer these questions:

1. How many jointed legs do the insects have?
2. How many body parts do they have?
3. Tap the insects lightly with your finger. Is the outside of their bodies hard or soft?
4. Do you have some insects with wings? Do you have some insects without wings?
5. Do you have some insects that fly, hop, or crawl?

Look back at the insects shown on pages 6 and 7. Are your insects like these? In what ways?

If you look closely at the heads of many insects, you will find different body parts.

Look at the different shapes of the **antennae** [an-TEHN-ee]. Long or short, thick or thin, all antennae help insects to sense the world that is around them. They help insects to sense each other, find food, and find the right direction.

Cecropia moth

Baltimore checkerspot

Milkweed beetle

Praying mantis

Apache wasp

Dragonfly

Gulf fritillary

Wasp

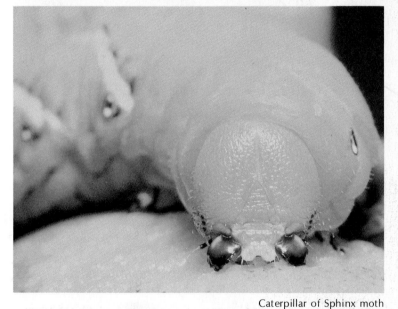
Caterpillar of Sphinx moth

Mosquito

Blowfly

Look at the different mouth parts of insects. Which insects do you think have mouth parts that suck the food? Which have mouth parts that bite food or chew it? Think of ways you take in food. You bite an apple and chew it. You drink a milkshake through a straw.

11

Deer fly

Insects can see almost all the way around them. Did you ever try to walk quietly up to a fly? When you had almost reached the fly, away it buzzed! A fly has two large eyes and three smaller ones in between. Using these eyes, the fly can see up, down, and all the way around. How do these eyes help the fly? Notice the large eyes of the fly in the picture. Find the eyes of a real fly, if you have one.

Can you see as far around as an insect? Here is a way to find out for yourself.

Look at something straight in front of you. Don't move your head or your eyes. Now stretch your right arm straight out in front of you.

Move only your fingers. You can see them move, of course. Now move your arm a little to the right, then more and more. Keep moving your fingers. When do you stop seeing your fingers?

Now try it with your left arm, moving to the left.

Now move your arm up, slowly, until you can't see it. Then move it down, lower and lower. How far can you see up, down, and to each side? Without moving your eyes or your head, can you see almost all the way around?

How Insects Grow and Change

Here is a picture of a young butterfly. It looks very different from an adult butterfly, doesn't it?

Monarch caterpillar

Monarch adult

Here is a picture of a baby and a man. In many ways the baby looks like the man, doesn't he?

Of course, people change as they grow, but they do not change as much as insects do. People get taller, fatter, or thinner, but they always have the same parts.

Most insects change three times before they become adults.

Growing in Four Stages

Most insects go through four stages as they grow:

1. Eggs are laid.

2. The eggs hatch into small wormlike animals called **larvae** [LAHR-vee]. One of these is called a larva. The larvae eat and grow. When they grow too big for their skins, they shed them. Some kinds of larvae shed their skins 10 or 12 times.

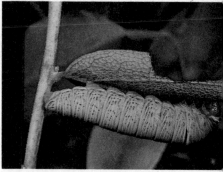

3. Now the larvae become **pupae** [PYOO-pee]. One of these is called a pupa. They stop eating and moving about. Many kinds of insects build a little case around themselves. While they are in their cases, the pupae change into adults. Finally, the cases split and the adult insects crawl out.

4. Now, at last, the insects are ready to begin their adult lives. The females lay eggs. What happens to the eggs after that?

The four growth stages of the Zebra swallowtail

You can see an insect going through some of its growing stages. You will need a liter jar, some soil, and a piece of cloth that has many tiny holes in it. Also get a rubber band, an egg carton, two bottle caps, and a metric ruler.

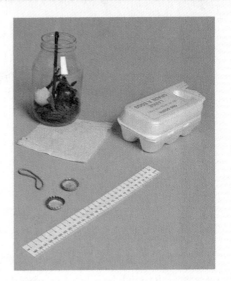

Put 3 cm of soil in the bottom of the jar. Go outside and look for insect larvae on the leaves of plants. Put them in the jar with the leaves and twigs that you found them on. Place the cloth over the jar and hold it in place with the rubber band. Feed the larvae often with more fresh leaves.

Look at the insects several times each week. Write down what is happening in the jar every time you look at it. Do you see the insects change size, shape, and color? Draw pictures of the insects as they change.

Cecropia caterpillar

When the larvae are fully grown, they will begin building cases where they change into pupae. Break part of the egg carton into small pieces and put the pieces in the jar. The larvae may make their cases on these pieces. Or they may make cases on the twigs or in the soil. At this time, the larvae stop eating. You should not feed the insects any more food until they crawl out of their cases.

Cecropia cocoon

If your jar is too dry, the pupae will die. Fill the bottle caps with water and place them in the jar. Sprinkle water on the soil only when it feels dry.

When the adults crawl out of their cases, be sure they have a twig to crawl onto. They will need to shake their wings. The adults also need room to fly and a place to find food. Now, open your jars outside and let the adults fly away.

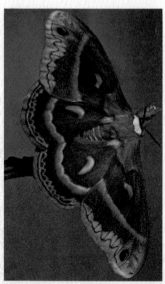

Male Cecropia moth

Growing in Three Stages

1. Some insects go through only three stages of growth. The young that are hatched from the eggs of this kind of insect are called **nymphs** [nimfs].

Milkweed bug eggs

2. Nymphs look much like their parents. But nymphs are smaller and have no wings. The nymphs eat and grow, shedding their skins when they outgrow them. In some grasshoppers, for example, this shedding happens five times.

Nymphs

3. At last the adult stage is reached. The females lay eggs. In your own words, tell what happens after that.

Adult

Why Are There So Many Insects?

Most insects have many enemies, and most insects are quite small. Think of all the kinds of big animals that you know. There are more kinds of insects in the world than all these big animals put together.

One reason there are so many insects is that they lay so many eggs. Another reason is that they are able to lay eggs in many different places. They lay their eggs in food, on roots, in water, and in clothing. Their eggs may also be found on other animals, on rocks, and under floors.

Aedes mosquito eggs on water

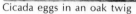
left: Aphids; right: Lady beetle eggs Cicada eggs in an oak twig

Braconid wasp eggs on a caterpillar

Another reason there are so many insects is that they have a very good sense of smell. They can smell food from far away. You smell odors with your nose. Insects use their antennae.

Here is a way to find out how well some insects can smell. You will need two jars, some foil, some clay, and two small pie pans. Also get a piece of ripe banana and a piece of raw beef.

Wrap each jar with foil and place three small lumps of clay on the edge of each jar. Put the piece of banana and the piece of beef in one jar. Leave the other jar empty. Place a pie pan upside down over the top of each jar. The lumps of clay will make a space between the jar tops and the pie pans.

Place the jars on the windowsill outside. Once in a while, look at them. Do you see any insects coming to the jar that has food in it? Could the insects see the food? How did they find the food?

Insects Have Ways of Finding Each Other

Even though male and female insects may be very far apart, they have ways of finding each other. They need to find one another so they can mate and make more of their own kind.

One way insects find one another is by smell. Scientists put a bit of special smell material from a female gypsy moth into a jar. They found that male moths flew to the jar from far away.

Another way is by hearing. Insects can hear each other. You have probably heard the call of the male katydid. It sounds like "Katy did, Katy did" over and over again. The male katydid calls until the female katydid finds him.

Male katydid

File and scraper on outer wings of male katydid

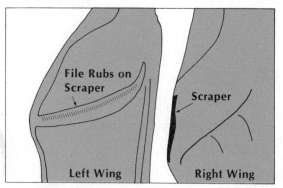

Male firefly beetle

The female firefly beetle
(glowworm) is wingless.

Some insects glow at night. Night is a good
time for insects to be out because most insect-
eaters are asleep. Insects such as the firefly can
find each other at night by glowing. Fireflies
have two special materials in their bodies. When
these materials come together, they give off
a glow.

Another way that insects find each other is by color, shape, and markings. Red, purple, orange, yellow—there are insects of every color. Some are striped; some have dots. Some insect colors and markings are very fancy. Would the males of any of these insects have any trouble finding females of the same kind?

Milkweed bugs

Bison stag beetles

Black swallowtail butterflies

Monarch butterflies

Color or Shape That Protects

Color works in other ways for insects. Insects are food for many birds, lizards, and other animals. Some insects have a color or shape that is hard to see. Which insects in the picture are hard to see because of their color? Which are hard to see because of their shape? Insects with special colors or shapes that keep them from being seen have a better chance of staying alive.

Measuring worm moth

Treehopper

Click beetle

Plant hopper

Katydid

Stick caterpillar

Nymphalidae cethosia

Insects That Work Together

You have seen how some insects have special ways of finding food, of finding each other, and of staying out of danger. Other insects live in a special way that is useful to them. They live together and share the work. These insects are called **social** [SOH-shuhl] insects. Ants, hornets, and honeybees are social insects. Let's find out how honeybees get their food.

Honeybees collect pollen from flowers.

Honeybees fly from flower to flower. At each stop, they drink a sweet liquid called **nectar** [NEHK-tuhr]. They put some **pollen** [PAHL-uhn] in the little pollen baskets on their legs. The pollen is a powder-like material found at the ends of the long stems in the flower.

Some of the pollen brushes off on other flowers and gets the flowers started in making seeds. The flowers have a lot of pollen. There is plenty of pollen for both the bees and the flowers.

Beehive

When the bees are loaded with nectar and pollen, they will fly back to the hive. Some of the nectar will be made into honey. Some of it will be mixed with pollen grains into "bee bread." Bread and honey—this is the food of bees.

The flowers may be far from their hive, yet the bees did not wander about looking for them. One bee found the flowers first and brought the good news to the rest of the hive.

The bee who looked for food did a special kind of dance. This dance told the other bees how far to fly and in what direction. The bees smelled the odor of the flowers as they buzzed around the dancing bee. Then they knew how far to fly, which way to fly, and what to look for.

left: Honeybee giving a message to other bees
below: Cells inside the hive

Off go those bees whose special work is getting nectar and pollen. All day long they work among the flowers. From the trees to the hive, they go back and forth all day long.

In the hive the nectar and pollen are made into honey and bee bread. The honey and bee bread are stored in six-sided spaces called cells. These cells are made of beeswax.

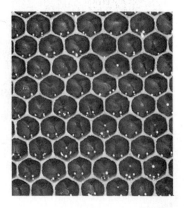

Bees inside the hive

There are many kinds of work to do in a bee-hive. The bees buzzing over you on summer days are probably worker bees looking for honey and pollen.

Back in the hive some of the bees are building the wax cells. Other bees keep the hive clean. There are bees that keep watch at the opening to the hive. They keep out any strange thing that might come in—even a bee from another hive.

Deep inside the hive is the queen bee. She is the mother of all the baby bees. Her work is to lay eggs in cell after cell of the hive. She does nothing but this very important work. Other worker bees feed her, and they keep her and the place around her clean.

left: Workers around the queen
below: Worker bees

These worker bees are feeding and cleaning the baby bees. Soon some of the baby bees will be workers. Some of the baby bees will become **drones** [drohnz]. Drones are male bees. One of them may become the father bee of a hive.

Bees live and work together to make a clean, safe home. Their young hatch and grow up safely inside the hive. The food that the worker bees find and store in the summer keeps all the bees fed through the winter. Dividing the work and sharing the food and home seems to work well for bees.

All ants divide their work and share their food. You can watch a group of ants living and working together. You will need a large widemouthed jar and a narrow jar of about the same height. Also get some thin cloth, black paper, tape, a rubber band, sugar, and some soil.

Place the smaller jar upside down inside the larger one. Fill the space between them with loose soil. With a small shovel, take the jar outdoors with you and look for an anthill. Dig up several ants from the anthill. Be sure to get a queen ant. The queen ant is bigger than the other ants. You may have to dig down deep to get the queen. Try to get some eggs and pupae too.

Put the ants into the jar. Cover the top of the jar with the cloth. Hold the cloth in place with a rubber band.

Since ants are used to living in dark places, wrap the piece of black paper around the jar and tape it. Take the paper off only when you want to look at them. The small jar will help to keep the ants near the sides of the large jar. This makes it easier to see the ants.

Feed the ants a little sugar each week. Put the sugar on top of the soil. Add a few drops of water to the soil each week. Make sure the soil does not dry out or get too soggy.

Look at the ants each day. Keep a record of what you see. What happens to the eggs, larvae, and pupae? Can you tell what different jobs the ants are doing? What kinds of things are happening in the jar?

Insect Pests

Some insects hurt food crops and other plants. It is very hard to get rid of insect pests when they find the right kind of food and place to live. Because it is so hard, farmers have called in scientists to help them get rid of these insects.

The scientists have tried many kinds of poison powders and liquids. They have pumped the poisons from tank trucks and sprayed them from airplanes. These poisons killed the insect pests, and the farmers' crops were saved. But using poisons raises many questions.

Spraying from the air

Spraying apple trees

In this picture you can see some apple trees being sprayed. Apple trees have many insect pests and farmers use many sprays to kill them. What, then, are some of the problems when these sprays are used?

1. Poisons may kill useful insects too. As you know, bees carry pollen from one apple flower to another. The apple flowers that are dusted with pollen start making seeds and fruit. What happens when the bees die?

2. Some sprays stay on the leaves. Later the leaves fall. They decay on the soil. What happens to the sprays?

3. Earthworms eat dead leaves. Some birds eat earthworms. Birds who eat many poisoned earthworms die of poison.

4. Without birds many more insects are able to live. Next year, the farmer will have to use more poisons or stronger poisons to control these insects.

5. The poisons that are sprayed to kill insects are also sprayed on the trees. Some of these poisons stay on the apples. These poisons are not good for people. What should you do with raw apples before eating them?

6. Suppose it rains. What is now in the water that runs off the land into streams?

7. Tell what you think happens to fish in this kind of stream. What might be happening to the men who spray?

Plants and animals need things from each other to grow and to stay alive. When one group is changed, this brings about other changes. Now, people are trying to get rid of certain insect pests without using poisons. For example, scientists have developed other ways of getting rid of cotton insect pests.

One way to get rid of these pests is to plant certain kinds of cotton that grow quickly. The pests don't have as much time to eat the cotton before it is picked.

Cotton harvester

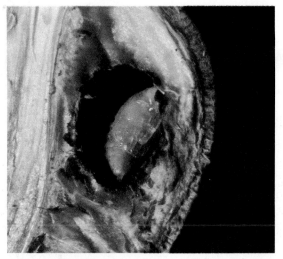

Boll weevil pupa   Boll weevil adult

Another way is to use special materials that scientists have made. These materials cause diseases that kill the harmful pests.

Assassin bug   Stink bug   Arabesque spider

The third way to get rid of cotton insect pests is to bring in animals that feed on them. Ants, spiders, and stink bugs are some of the animals that eat cotton insect pests.

It takes a long time to return a place to what it was before poisons were used. Now, scientists and farmers are working together to develop even more ways of getting rid of pests.

Fire ants

35

What Did You Learn?

- Insects can be found almost anywhere on Earth.
- All adult insects have six jointed legs, three body parts, and an outside skeleton.
- Many insects may have special head parts: antennae, mouth parts for sucking and chewing, and eyes that see almost all the way around.
- Most insects go through four stages of growth: eggs, larvae, pupae, and adults.
- Some insects go through only three stages of growth: eggs, nymphs, and adults.
- There are many kinds of insects because they lay many eggs in many different places.
- Some insects find each other by making sounds or by glowing.
- Some insects have a color or shape that protects them from being eaten.
- Insects that live together and share the work are called social insects.
- Poisons that are used to get rid of insect pests may cause harmful changes in soil, water, and living things.

Career

Beekeeper

There are more insects than all other animals in the world. Not all insects are helpful to us, but the honeybee is. It carries pollen from flower to flower and also gives us honey and beeswax.

Beekeepers in the United States take care of about four million hives. They must handle their bees carefully so the bees won't sting them. If the beekeeper moves very slowly, the bees will not be bothered. Beekeepers wear netted hats to protect their faces. But most of them don't wear gloves because they get sticky from the honey.

To collect the honey, beekeepers first blow smoke into the hive to quiet the bees. Then the trays filled with honey are removed. A machine drains the honey from the trays and prepares it for use. Bakers use honey in making crackers, cookies, and other baked goods. The beeswax from which the cells of the hive are made is used in candles, polishes, and other things.

TO THINK ABOUT AND DO

WORD FUN

Copy and complete each sentence on a piece of paper.

1. The body parts of adult insects are the
   _____, _____, and _____.
2. The special head parts of many insects are
   _____, _____, and _____.
3. The four stages of growth of most insects
   are _____, _____, _____, and _____.
4. Insects may find each other by making
   sounds or by _____.
5. Insects that live and work together are
   _____ insects.
6. Some harmful changes in the earth and in
   living things may be caused by _____ that
   are used to kill insect pests.

WHAT DO YOU REMEMBER?

Write these sentences on a piece of paper.
Write **T** for the sentences that are true and **F** for
the sentences that are false.

1. Insects are found almost everywhere on the earth.
2. Some insects go through two stages of growth.
3. Color or shape of the insect may protect it from
   being eaten.
4. There are many insects because they lay so
   many eggs.

Some of the animals in the pictures are not insects. Tell why they are not insects.

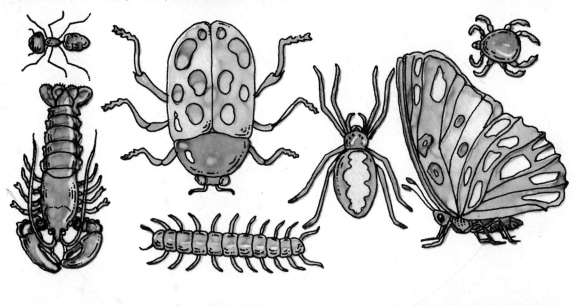

Have you ever heard a cricket chirp? Crickets chirp when the temperature is between 10° C and 40° C.

Crickets chirp by rubbing two parts of their bodies together. The higher the temperature, the faster the crickets chirp. You can find out the temperature by counting the number of chirps.

To find the temperature, count the number of chirps in 15 seconds. Then add 5. Multiply the sum by 5. Then divide by 9. That number is the temperature in degrees Celsius at the cricket's location. What is the temperature if a cricket chirps 40 times in 15 seconds?

Unit 11

Structures
Make Work Easier

Machines and Force 2

Have you ever played tug-of-war like these boys and girls? Your team tries to pull the other team across the line. You use your hands and arms to pull the rope. You can feel your feet push and move against the ground as you try to win the game. Will your team win the tug-of-war?

An object may move when something else pushes or pulls it. Your team is winning because everyone is pulling the other team across the line. The push or pull that can cause something to move is called a **force** [fohrs].

photo at left: Tug-of-war

Forces

You use a force whenever you push the pedals of your bicycle or kick a ball. Look at the pictures. What forces are causing these things to move?

The members of one team in the tug-of-war game are pulling in one direction. The members of the other team are also pulling in one direction. But the two teams are pulling on the rope in opposite directions. These forces are acting against each other. What will happen if each team pulls with the same amount of force? Will one team be able to win by pulling the other team over the line?

What happens when objects are pulled from both sides with equal and unequal forces? You will need two spring scales, five books, and some string.

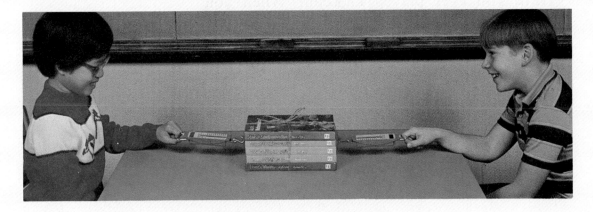

Tie the books together with the string. Attach both spring scales to the books. Have each person pull with a force of one **newton** [NOOT-n]. Do the books move? Each of you has pulled with equal force. In what direction is each of you pulling? How would you describe what happens when an object is pulled with equal forces but in opposite directions?

What would happen if one pull or force is greater than the other? Have one person pull the books with a force of five newtons. Have the other person pull with a force of one newton. The books are being pulled in opposite directions but with different amounts of force. Do the books move? In which direction do they move?

In the tug-of-war game, the winning team used a greater force to move the other team over the line. The losing team was moved in the direction of this greater force. If each team pulls with exactly the same force, there will be a tie.

Have you ever played kickball? When you kick, you use force to start the ball moving. You use force to slow down and stop things, too. When you play kickball, you use force to catch and stop the ball. People use force to make things stop, start, speed up, and slow down.

The forces from these machines are used in different ways. Find the machine that is used to lift something. Find the machine that is being used to pull something. Which machine is pushing something?

A Board and Block That Lifts Things

To move something you must use force. You would need a lot of force to lift this full-grown man all by yourself. Your muscles alone do not have enough strength to do it. But you can use a machine like this one to help you lift the man.

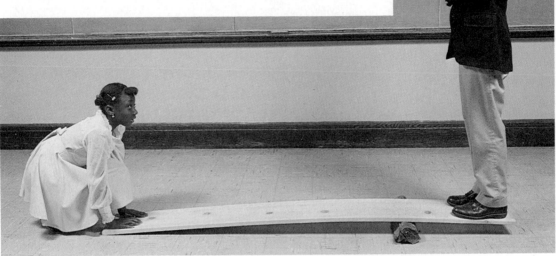

Using a lever

A board and a block used in this way is a machine. This kind of machine is called a **lever** [LEHV-uhr]. There are many kinds and shapes of levers, but all levers have three parts.

The **fulcrum** [FUHL-kruhm] is the turning point about which a lever moves. The fulcrum itself usually does not move. The force arm is the distance from the force to the fulcrum. The load arm is the distance from the fulcrum to the load.

Notice that the fulcrum is near the load. Does it make a difference where you put the fulcrum? Would it be easier to lift the man if you moved the fulcrum to the middle of the board?

Here is a way to find out how levers work. Fill a milk carton with sand. Then set up a meterstick, a spring scale, the carton, some string, and a book in this way.

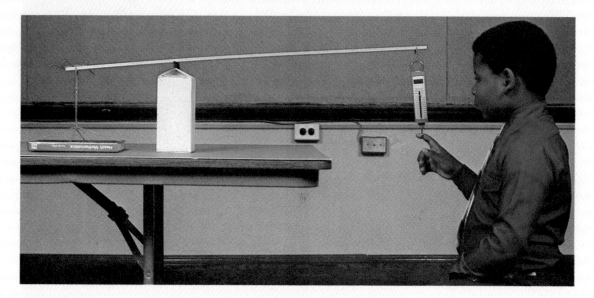

The book is the load you are going to lift. When the fulcrum is at the 15-cm mark, how long is the force arm? How long is the load arm? Copy the chart and write your findings on it.

Use the end of the spring scale to slowly pull down the end of the meterstick. How much force does it take to lift the book?

Now move the fulcrum to the 20-cm mark and lift the book. How long is the force arm? How long is the load arm? How much force does it take to lift the book? Write your findings in your chart.

Move the fulcrum to each of the three other centimeter marks. For each position of the fulcrum, find the amount of force needed to lift the book. Be sure to write in your chart the lengths of the load and force arms, as well as the force.

When you finish, look at your chart. When did you use less force to lift the book? Did you need less force when the load arm was longer or when the force arm was longer? You saw that the lever made it easier to lift the book.

Fulcrum at	Length of Force Arm	Length of Load Arm	Force Needed (Newtons)
15 Centimeters			
20 Centimeters			
25 Centimeters			
30 Centimeters			
35 Centimeters			

The closer the fulcrum is to the load, the easier it is to lift the load.

Depending on what we need to do, we use levers in many different ways. The levers in the picture look quite different from one another, but they all make work easier.

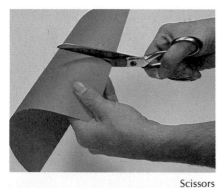

Scissors

Seesaw

Pruning shears

Pry bar

Look at how these levers are being used. Which ones are really made of two levers that cross over each other? Where is the fulcrum of each lever?

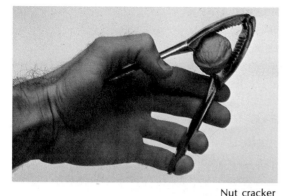
Nut cracker

Can opener

Sugar tongs

Tweezers

Here are four levers whose fulcrums are at one end, rather than between the force and the load. The fulcrum of the nutcracker is easy to see. It is the hinge where the two parts of the nutcracker meet.

The can opener, too, has its fulcrum at the hinge where its two parts meet. How about the sugar tongs and the tweezers? Think of how you open and close them. Which part does not move? That part is the fulcrum.

Look around and you will see levers being used everywhere. With a lever you can move things more easily than you can without it. Machines such as levers make our work easier.

A Machine Made from a Sloping Board

You cannot possibly find a machine that is any simpler than this one. It is just a sloping board with one end higher than the other. It is used for many jobs in which heavy things have to be lifted. A board used in this way is called an **inclined plane** [ihn-KLYND playn]. Inclined means sloping. A plane is a flat surface. How do you think the woman is using an inclined plane?

An inclined plane

Let's find out how an inclined plane can help us. You will need a spring scale, a few books, a board, and a metal toy truck or wagon.

Hang the toy truck on the scale. Then lift the toy truck with the spring scale. Does the truck feel heavy? With how much force does it pull on the scale?

Make an inclined plane with the board and the books. Pull the toy up the inclined plane. Now how much force are you using to pull the toy? Do you need as much force as when you pulled the toy straight up?

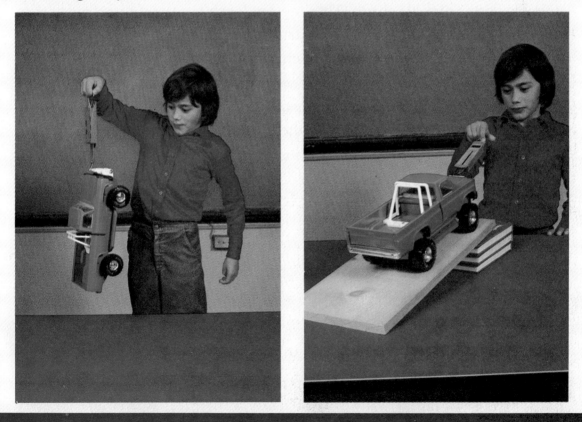

With an inclined plane you use less force to move an object than when you pull the object straight up.

Inclined planes are a great help in many jobs. The ramps in garages, gas stations, and many buildings are really inclined planes. People in wheelchairs use inclined planes to move about more easily. Where have you seen people using inclined planes this way?

Sometimes an inclined plane is not shaped in a straight line. For example, let's look at a mountain road.

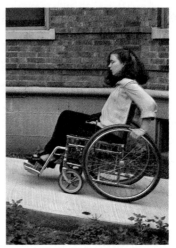

A ramp is an inclined plane.

The mountain in the first picture is much too steep for any truck to climb. The engine doesn't have enough force to push a heavy truck straight up the mountain. However, we can cut a winding road into the mountain, as in the second picture. This winding road is really an inclined plane that turns around on itself. It makes the mountain much less steep to climb. A truck can climb such a road, because less force is needed.

Which road is easier to climb?

Let's find out how much less force is needed when the road is made less steep. You will need a spring scale, a wooden board, some books, and a heavy metal toy truck or wagon.

Pile up enough books to make a steep road. Use the spring scale to pull the toy up the inclined plane. How much force did it take? Then take away some of the books to make the road less steep and try it again. Keep a record of your findings. What did you find out?

Holding and Splitting Things

Every day you see a different kind of inclined plane, but it doesn't look like one. You can find it in chairs, tools, and many toys. It is called a **screw** [skroo].

Let's see how a screw is really an inclined plane. You will need a piece of paper, scissors, a crayon, and a pencil.

Cut a piece of paper into this shape ◿ . Which edge of the paper has the shape of an inclined plane? Mark both sides of this edge with a crayon. Roll the paper around a pencil. When you are finished, what does the edge look like?

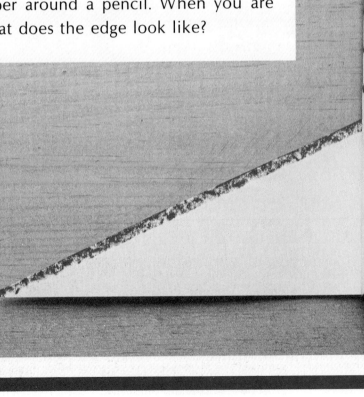

A screw is really a curved inclined plane. We use these curved inclined planes to help us in many ways. The force of your hands cannot hold two pieces of wood tightly together. Yet the same kind of force can be used to turn a tool that then turns a screw. The screw pulls the two pieces together very tightly.

Wood screw fastening two pieces of wood

The force you can make with your arms cannot lift a car. Yet you can use the same force to turn the handle of a jackscrew and lift the car quite easily.

Jackscrew

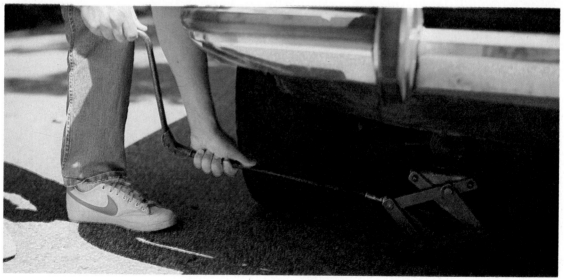

A **wedge** [wehj] looks like an inclined plane, but it helps make work easier in a somewhat different way. A wedge helps you cut things apart when the force of your arms alone is not great enough. With a wedge called an ax, you use a force to split a thick piece of wood. If you used the same force but without the ax, you could not split the wood. Look at an ax from the end and you will see that it has the shape of two inclined planes put together.

Using a wedge

Anything in these shapes is a wedge. Many kinds of wedges are used for cutting and splitting things. They have many different shapes, but they all act in the same way.

Hand Rake

Cold Chisel

Chisel

Pocket Knife

You can find out more about how a wedge works. Get a piece of thick cardboard, scissors, some sand, and a metric ruler.

Cut the cardboard into a wedge about 12 cm long and 8 cm wide. Push this wedge through some sand. Which way does the sand move? Measure how far the sand is pushed to each side.

Each kind of wedge has a sharp edge that cuts through material, and a thicker part that spreads the material apart. The wedge can split a piece of wood or move snow from a road. In these ways, the wedge can make work easier.

Raising Things More Easily

Have you ever helped raise a flag at school or at camp? Try to think of a way of raising a flag to the top of the pole without using the rope. You could climb the pole to raise the flag. But it would be very hard work. It's much easier to use a wheel with a rope moving over it. The wheel and rope are used together as a **pulley** [PUHL-ee].

Notice the pulley in the picture. It is a kind of wheel that turns about an **axle** [AK-suhl]. Since the pulley is fastened to the pole, it is called a fixed pulley. As you pull down on the rope, the flag goes up the pole. With a fixed pulley, you can lift the flag without climbing the pole.

One use of a pulley

The fixed pulley is used to change the direction of the force. As the boy pulls down on the rope, in what direction will his pail move? How does this help him?

Sometimes a pulley also moves as you move a heavy load. This kind of pulley is a movable pulley. It moves along the rope with the load. The movable pulley is usually used together with the fixed pulley to make the work easier.

top left: Double pulley; *bottom left:* Pulley for dinghy; *above:* Pulley rig on crane

61

Let's find out more about a movable pulley. You will need a pail, some sand, two pulleys, a long rope, a short rope, and a spring scale.

Put some sand in a pail. Attach the spring scale to the handle of the pail and lift it. How much force is needed to lift the pail? Then lift the pail with the pulleys, as the girl is doing here. Now, how much force is needed to lift the pail?

When you use a movable pulley in this way, you can lift a much heavier load than usual. The reason is that you are holding up only half the load with your end of the rope. What is holding up the other half? The pulley fastened to the load also moves up and down with it.

With more pulleys you can lift still heavier loads. Here you see pulleys being used for lifting a heavy box. Can you find a fixed pulley? Can you find a movable pulley? To which pulley is the box attached?

Can you find the fixed and movable pulleys?

Notice how the ropes pass back and forth between the wheels. As the rope is pulled down, the lower pulley and box move up. By using pulleys in this way, you can lift a very heavy load. This girl is lifting almost four times the weight she could lift with a single fixed pulley.

Things That Turn Together

Here is a different kind of machine. It has a wheel that is fastened to an axle. The wheel and axle turn together. There is a wheel and axle on a radio, on a television, and even on a door. When the wheel is turned, it turns the axle, and the axle turns something else. In the radio and television the axle turns a part that tunes in the station. The doorknob's axle turns a part that opens the door.

Wheels and axles

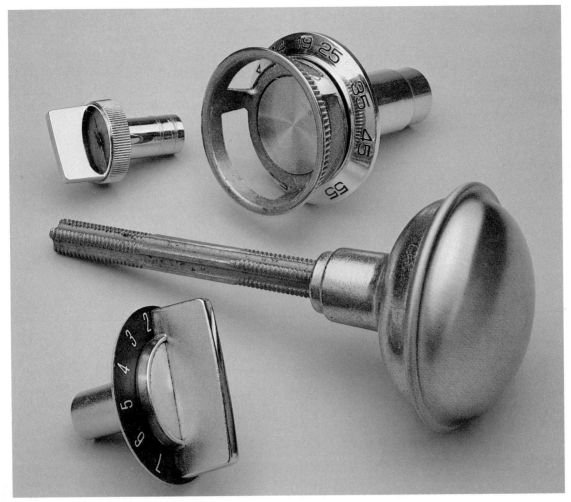

64

Let's find out how a wheel and axle make work easier. You will need a milk carton, sand, a pencil, a spool that fits tightly on the pencil, some string, tape, and a book.

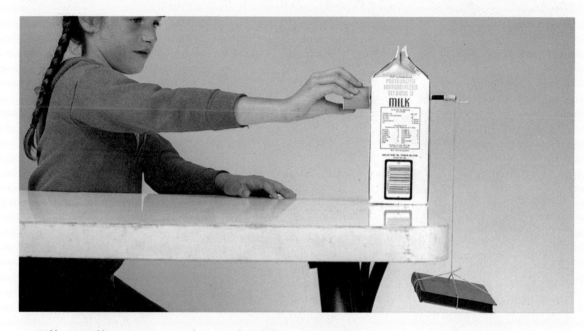

Fill a milk carton with sand. Then, near the top of the carton, make two holes that the pencil can pass through. Turn the pencil until it moves freely.

After fastening the string to the book, tie and tape the other end tightly to the pencil. Try to lift the book by turning the pencil with your fingers.

Now push the spool onto the pencil. Be sure it fits tightly. Turn the spool and again try to lift the book. Is it easier now?

What part is the wheel? What part is the axle?

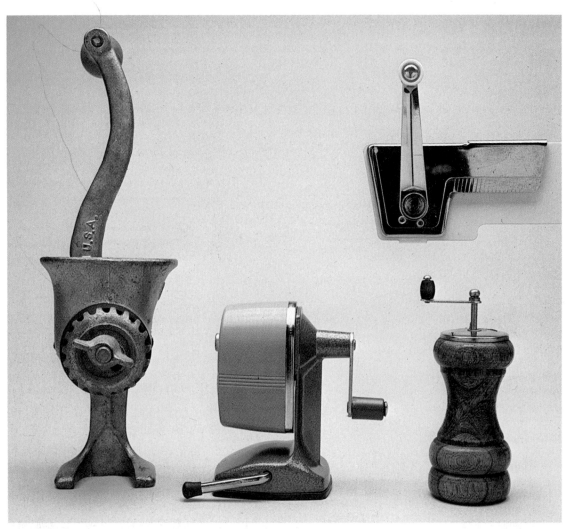

Have you used any of these wheels and axles?

We use a wheel and axle in many ways to make work easier. Where is the wheel in each of the machines above? Do you see that the handle is really one spoke of the wheel? In each machine you turn a handle that is fastened to an axle. The turning axle works another part inside the machine. Could you turn the axle of a meat grinder or a pencil sharpener without the handle?

Dragging and Pulling Back

This big load of logs must be moved! But it's much too heavy for a person to move without help. This person is using the large tractor to help him move the logs. Why is so much force needed to move this load? The load is slowed down as it moves over the rough, bumpy ground. This dragging and pulling back on the load is called **friction** [FRIHK-shuhn].

A logging tractor

Here is a way to find out more about friction. You will need five books, some string, a spring scale, a sheet of sandpaper, and a cotton ball.

Tie the books together with the string. Put the pile of books on the sandpaper. Attach the spring scale to the string.

Pull the books across the sandpaper with the spring scale. How much force is needed to move the books?

Now put the books on the smooth desk and do it again. Do you need the same force to move them?

You can do something else to see why it takes more force to pull a load over a rough surface than over a smooth surface. Use the sandpaper again and rub the cotton across it. What do you see on the sandpaper? Do the rough places on the sandpaper catch, drag, and tear the cotton?

Whenever two things rub against each other, there is some friction. Smooth surfaces make less friction than rough surfaces, however. This is because rough surfaces pull back and drag more than smooth surfaces.

Press your foot against the floor and push it forward. Feel the force you need. Where is the friction? Tell which of these shoes makes more friction with the floor.

Getting Rid of Friction

Every time you move something you have to work against friction. If you could get rid of some friction, you would need less force to move something.

Press your hand against your desk and push forward. Feel how much force you need. Where is the friction? Wet your hand and try it again. Now there is a liquid between your hand and the desk. Is more or less force needed now?

Lubrication [loo-bruh-KAY-shuhn] is getting rid of some friction by using a material such as water or oil. Lubrication makes a surface get slippery. Other materials can also be used to get rid of some friction. They are put between surfaces that rub together. Where have you seen these things being used?

Things used to lubricate

Suppose we could get rid of all friction. Do you think this would be a good idea? Wouldn't it make the work you have to do in moving something very, very easy?

ACTIVITY

What happens when we remove some of the friction? Try this and see.

You will need a jar with a cover that screws on, some soap, and some water.

Screw the cover on the jar as tightly as you can. Then unscrew it. Then tighten it again. Now wet your hands with soapy water. Try to unscrew the jar cap. Is it easy to unscrew the cap? The soapy water got rid of a lot of friction. What do we call this use of the soapy water?

Look at the picture. The arrows point to places where there is friction. Tell what would happen at each place if there were no friction. If you could get rid of all friction, would you do it?

Every day friction is useful to you in many different ways. You are able to walk because there is friction between your shoes and the ground. Think about how you slip and slide with new shoes on a smooth floor or on ice.

Without some friction the wheels of a car would spin without moving the car. If somehow the car did get moving, you would really be in trouble, because you could not stop. The brakes of a car are made of materials that stop the wheels by friction. Also, the tires are made to grip the road.

Have you seen brakes like these on bicycles? How do they use friction?

Bicycle hand brake

What Did You Learn?

- A force is any push or pull.
- Objects do not move when equal forces act on them from opposite directions.
- Objects move in the direction of greater force when unequal forces act on them from opposite directions.
- A force can change the speed and direction in which things are moving.
- Levers, inclined planes, screws, wedges, wheels and axles, and pulleys are machines that make work easier.
- Friction occurs when two things rub against each other.
- Lubrication helps to get rid of some friction.
- Friction is useful to us in many different ways because it helps us to control movement.

Career

Construction Worker

Do you like to work with machines, take things apart, or find out how things work? Then you might enjoy working with machines as construction workers do.

People have used machines to build with for thousands of years. They found they could use logs fastened to inclined planes to drag large stone blocks. These people used levers to move the heavy blocks into place. Then they used wedges to cut the stone blocks into the needed shapes. Today, new ways and modern machines are used to build tall and small buildings.

Have you seen a building being built by construction workers? Often construction companies build a fence around their projects so that no one will be hurt. But many people like to watch the workers, and so the workers put windows in the fences. If you have ever looked through these windows or visited a construction area, you may have seen many workers and machines. Did you watch the workers put sides on the building, hammer a floor in place, and drive large machines? Construction workers are trained to use many machines that make work easier and faster.

TO THINK ABOUT AND DO

The arrows on each picture tell about machines and force. On a piece of paper write the answer that belongs in each circle. Choose your answers from the list of words below.

wedge

screw

pulley

wheel and axle

Write these sentences on a piece of paper. Write **T** for the sentences that are true and **F** for the sentences that are false.

1. Machines help people do many jobs that they could not do by using their muscles alone.
2. If equal forces act on an object from opposite directions, the object will move.
3. Lubrication is used to make objects move more easily by getting rid of some of the friction.
4. You need some friction to walk and to ride your bicycle safely.
5. An inclined plane is a slanted surface that helps you move objects with less force.

GETTING THE JOB DONE

What machines are needed to do the work in this picture? On a piece of paper write the names of the machines and the kinds of jobs they do.

ACTIVITY

Let's find out how rollers help us get rid of some friction. Get three pencils, five books, and some string.

Tie the books together. Pull this load across the table. Is it easy or hard to pull? Now put the pencils under the books. You will be using the pencils as rollers. Pull the load across the table. How does it feel to pull the load now? Take the rollers away and try again. Is it easier or harder? How do rollers get rid of some friction?

HOW WERE THESE BUILT?

These pyramids were built thousands of years ago. They are square on the bottom and have four sides that come to a point at the top. Find out how they were built and who built them. What machines were used?

Bones and Muscles

3

What are the people doing in the picture? Have you ever seen a house being built? Many pieces of wood are nailed together to build this house. The framework is built first to give the house support.

In some ways your body is like the house. Your many bones fit together to make the framework of your body. Just as a wooden framework supports the house, your framework of bones supports your body.

photo at left: Framing a house

Bones Support and Protect

Your framework is made up of many bones—there are more than 200 of them in all! One of the most important things that your bones do is to support you. Bones are like the wooden framework of the house. The walls, floors, ceilings, and other parts of the house are supported by the wooden framework. Your heart, stomach, muscles, skin, and other parts are supported by your bony framework, your skeleton. Without a skeleton for support, you couldn't stand up or even sit up straight.

Another thing your bones do is to protect the important organs of your body. Look at the picture of the skeleton. As you read further, you will learn the names of many of these bones.

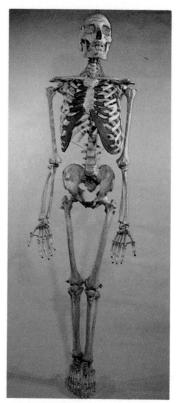

Human skeleton

Use your fingers to feel the bone that gives your head its shape. This is called the **skull** [skuhl]. The top of the skull feels like one large bone, but it is really eight bones that have grown together. When you were born, the eight bones were separate. In the first year or two of your life, the skull bones grew together. Your skull is like a strong, built-in helmet. It protects your brain from bumps and bruises. What other body parts does it protect?

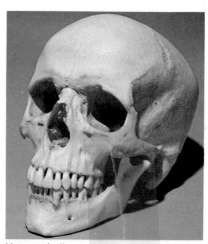

Human skull

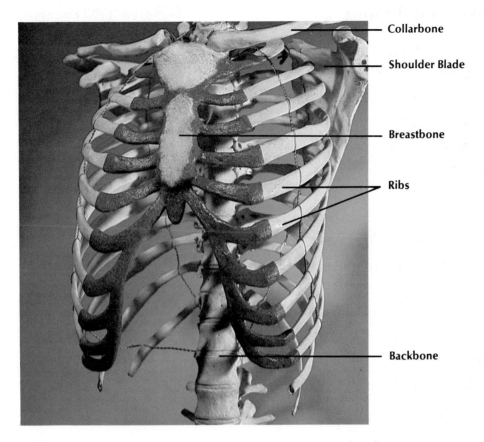

Collarbone

Shoulder Blade

Breastbone

Ribs

Backbone

Many other bones help to protect your body. Place your hands on the sides of your chest. What do you feel? The bones you feel are called **ribs.**

Your ribs make a shape like a cage. Look at the picture and find out which bone forms the front of the rib cage. Feel this bone with your fingers. What bone forms the back of the cage? Use the picture to help you find out.

Put your hand on your chest. Do you feel the beating of your heart? The heart is protected by the rib cage. What other body parts are protected by the rib cage?

Feel the bones in the middle of your back. Do they feel bumpy or smooth? Are they hard? You are feeling some of the bones in your backbone. The backbone is made up of 33 bones that form a long tube.

below: One bone from the backbone

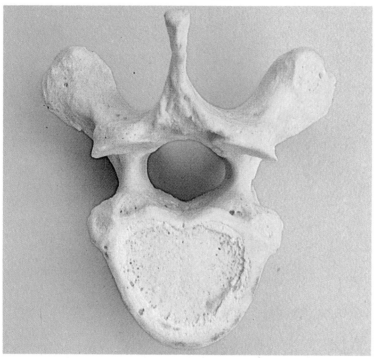

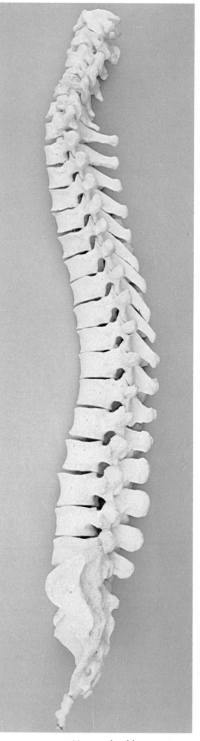

Here is a bone from the backbone. Look at the hole in it. A thin ropelike part goes through this hole. How do you think the backbone protects this part of your body?

The bones in your back also help you stand up straight. At the same time, they allow you to bend and stoop, twist and turn. Without a backbone for support, you couldn't stand up and you wouldn't even be able to sit up straight. The backbone is the chief body support.

Human backbone

Bones of Many Sizes and Shapes

Did you know that you were only about 45 cm long when you were born? Today you may be almost as tall as your parents. You may weigh more than ten times as much as you did when you were born.

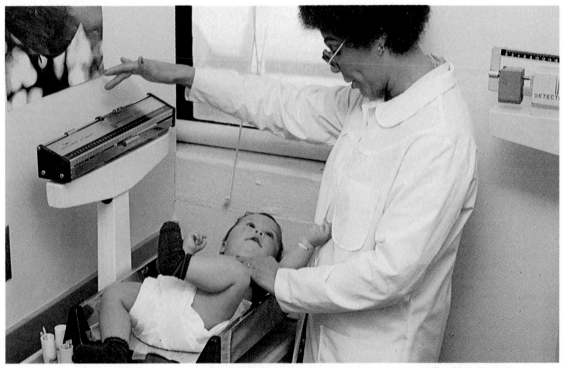

Checking the baby's weight

In one year you may grow a lot, while there may be very little change in the next year. The girls in your grade may grow faster than the boys. Later, the boys begin to catch up and grow taller than most of the girls. When you measure your gain in height, you are really measuring how much longer your skeleton has grown. How tall are you now?

Here's a way to measure the length of your skeleton. You will need a piece of paper, some tape, and a meterstick.

Stand straight against a wall in your classroom. Have a friend tape a piece of paper to the wall, behind your head. Then have your friend place the meterstick lightly on top of your head. Ask your friend to make a mark on the paper where the meterstick touches it.

Use the meterstick to measure the distance from the floor to the mark on the paper. How tall are you?

Now, have your friend stand against the wall and measure your friend's height.

Do the boys or the girls have the longer skeletons? You need to make a chart like this one to find out. Write the height of each boy and girl on the chart. Your teacher will add up all the boys' heights and divide that sum by the number of boys in the class. What is the average height of the boys? Your teacher will do the same thing with the girls' heights. What is their average height? Compare the two numbers to see if boys or girls have longer skeletons.

Length of Skeleton in Centimeters

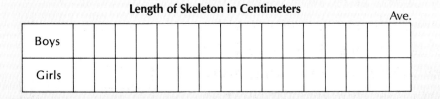

												Ave.
Boys												
Girls												

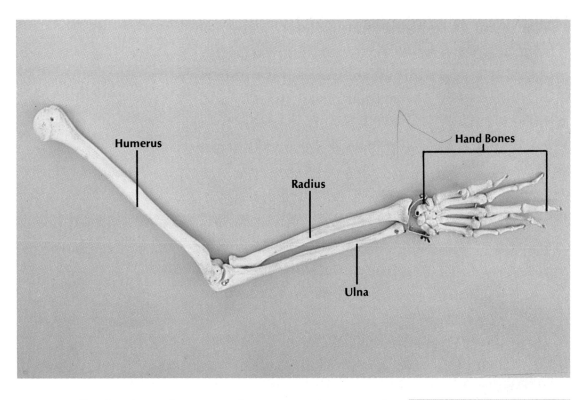

Humerus

Radius

Hand Bones

Ulna

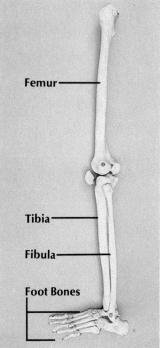

Femur

Tibia

Fibula

Foot Bones

Your body has bones of many sizes and shapes. Feel the bones in your arm. Some of the bones in your hands are so tiny they can't be felt. Your arm goes from the shoulder to the fingertips. There are 32 bones in each arm. How many of them can you feel with your fingers? Name the three large, long bones in your arm.

Your leg goes from your hip to your toes. Each leg has 31 bones. Measure the long bone that goes from your hip to the knee. As you measure the length of your leg, place the metric ruler along the outside of your leg. How long is it? When you were a tiny baby, your arms were longer than your legs. Are your arms longer than your legs now?

When you were born, your skeleton wasn't as hard as it is now. As you grow, most of the softer material is replaced by bone. Bones have minerals in them that make them hard, tough, and strong. What do you think would happen to a bone if some of the minerals were taken out of it?

ACTIVITY

Let's find out what happens to bones if some of the minerals are removed. You will need two chicken leg bones, some water, some soap, some vinegar, and two jars.

Wash the bones with soap and water. Put one bone in a jar filled with vinegar. Vinegar removes some of the minerals in the bone. Put the other bone in a jar filled with water. Leave the bones in the jars for about seven days.

Again, wash the bones with soap and water. Look at the bones. Are both bones still hard? Have they changed shape? What happens to bones if minerals are removed?

The outer part of a bone is hard, tough, and strong. Does this mean that a bone can support any force put on it, even a very great force? If you have ever broken a bone, you know that it can't.

left: X ray of broken bone
right: X ray of same bone after it has mended
bottom: A plaster cast helps keep the broken bone in place.

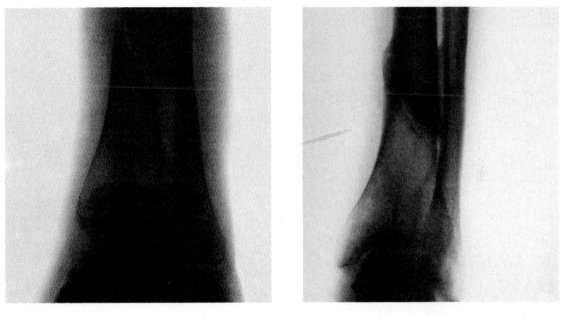

When a bone is broken, your body makes new bone material in and around the break. This material repairs the break and mends the pieces together. This part of your skeleton becomes as strong as before or even stronger.

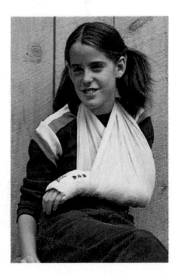

Think about what would happen if the bone were not put in exactly the same place. The bone would heal in the wrong place and wouldn't fit together with the other bones. That is why a broken bone must be held in place for about two months while it is being repaired. Have you ever broken a bone? How did it happen?

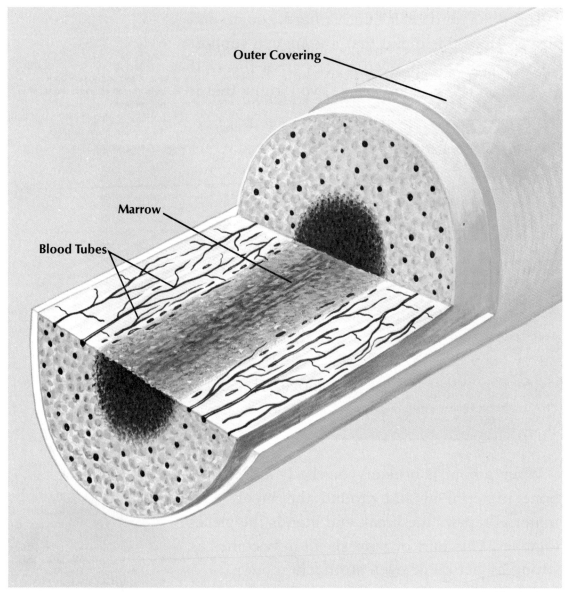

Outer Covering

Marrow

Blood Tubes

Inside of a bone

Bones do something else besides supporting and protecting you. Some bones make parts of your blood. They do this in the part of the bone called the **marrow** [MAR-oh]. The marrow fills a space in the middle of the bone. Around the marrow is the hard mineral part of the bone.

Bones Joining Together

Your skeleton is like the framework of a building. Yet it is much more than that. A building stays in place. The parts of its framework are fastened together so they barely move. But you want to walk, jump, bend, and make many different kinds of movements. Your skeleton supports and protects you, not only when you stand still, but when you move around. Let's find out how the parts of your skeleton are able to move.

Feel the bone that goes from your foot to your knee. It is a hard, firm bone that can support the weight of your body. It joins another bone that goes from your knee to your hip. This bone, too, is hard and firm. Yet the place where the two bones meet at your knee can move. The place where bones come together is called a **joint** [joynt].

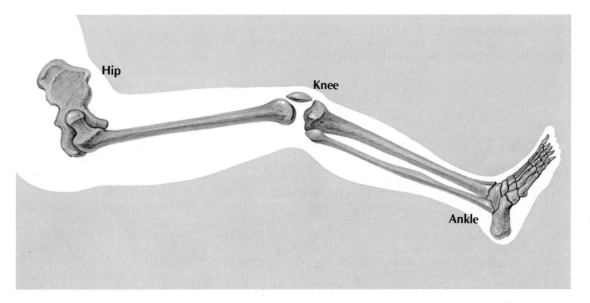

You can swing your leg back and forth because your knee joint works like a door hinge. In your elbow there is another joint that works like a hinge. It lets you move the lower part of your arm without moving the upper part.

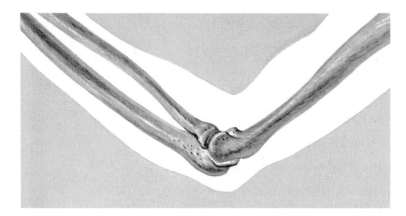

Elbow joint

Put your elbow on the desk and let your arm drop down onto the desk. Lift your arm without raising your elbow. Can your arm move up and down?

Move your fingers, toes, and ankles. In which directions can you move them? Notice that they can only move back and forth like a hinge.

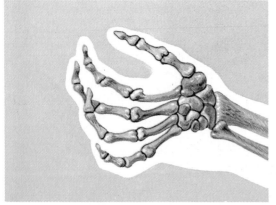

Fingers and wrist

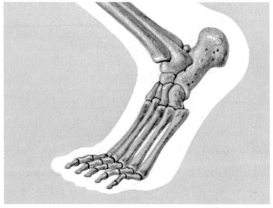

Ankle and toes

Some of your bones are able to move back and forth. They can also move left and right, and even in a circle. This kind of joint is called a ball-and-socket. In this joint, the end of one bone is shaped like a ball. The ball fits an open socket in the other bone.

Shoulder joint   Hip joint

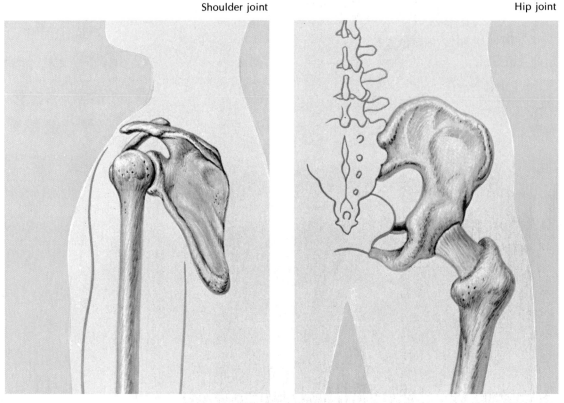

Your arms are joined to your shoulders by ball-and-socket joints. Your legs are joined to your hips in the same way. Can you describe what happens in these joints when you throw a ball? When you catch a ball? When you run? When you dance? How would these actions be different if you had hinge joints in your hips and shoulders?

Your bones are joined in other ways, too. The joint in your wrist is a sliding joint. The many small bones in your wrist slide over each other. Try wiggling your wrist to see how it works. It can move up and down, back and forth, in different directions.

Still another kind of joint is the pivot joint. It lets you turn one part of your body without moving the part it is connected to. Turn your head. The joint between your head and neck acts as a pivot.

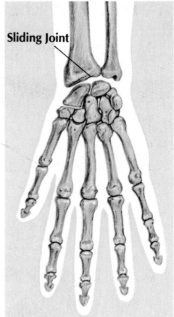

Sliding Joint

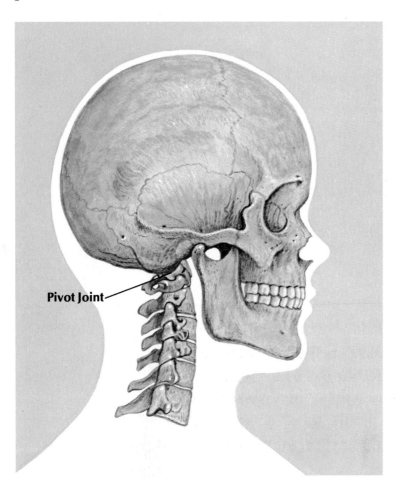

Pivot Joint

A Closer Look at a Joint

Your joints must be easy to move but not too loose. They also must be strong and wear a long time. In a joint, the ends of the bones that rub together are larger than the rest of the bones. The ends are covered with a smooth material called **cartilage** [KAHR-tl-ihj]. Cartilage is a strong material that protects the ends of your bones.

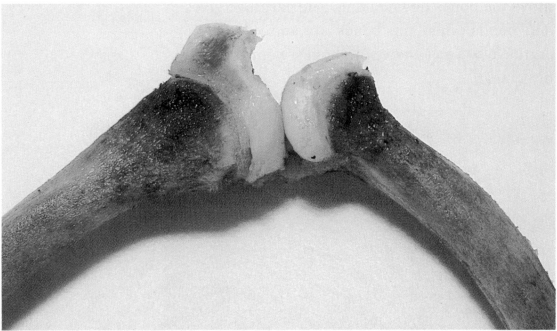

Cartilage protects the ends of bones.

Think about what would happen if cartilage weren't in your joints. You could probably hear and feel the bones rubbing against each other every time you moved. What might happen to the bones if they kept rubbing against one another?

There is much more cartilage between the bones in your ribs and back than between other bones. The cartilage between the bones in your back lets you bend more easily. It makes the backbone more springy. The cartilage also stops the bones from rubbing against each other.

Feel the bone in the middle of your chest. Cartilage fastens most of your ribs to this bone. When you breathe, the muscles in your chest move these bones up and out. Then the muscles move the bones down and in. The cartilage gives and bends when the bones are moved. If the cartilage weren't there, the bones would probably crack.

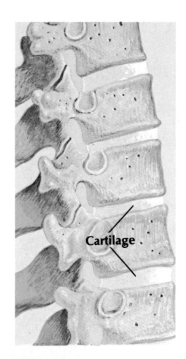

Cartilage

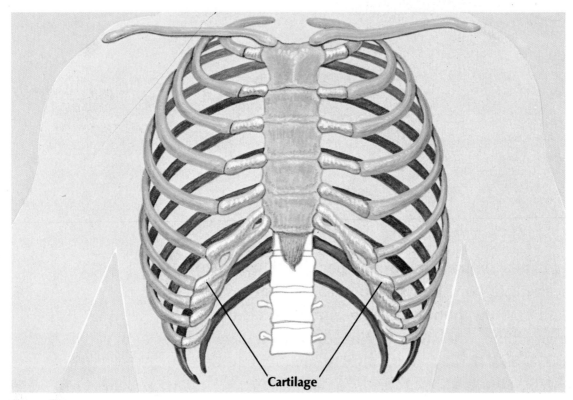

Cartilage

You can measure how much the rib cage is moved during breathing.

Put a metric tape measure around a person's chest. Measure the size of the chest when the person breathes in deeply. Have the person breathe out. Measure the chest again. How many centimeters does this person's ribs move? Now, have that person do the same thing to you.

The chest muscles moved the rib cage during breathing. Cartilage bent back and forth when air came into the body and when it was pushed out.

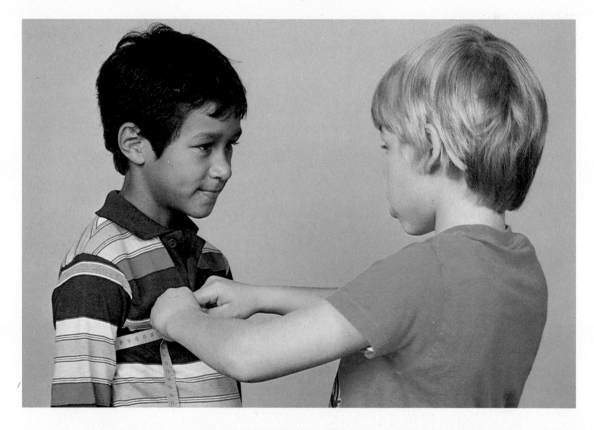

Cartilage in your nose, throat, and ears gives them shape and holds them up. Place your hand on your ear and move your ear around. Feel how easily the cartilage bends.

If you look closely at the ends of the bones below, you will see long cords. These cords are some of the toughest material in your body. They are called **ligaments** [LIHG-uh-muhnts]. Ligaments tie the bones together at the joints. Think about how hard your joints are used. The ligaments must be very strong. They must keep the bones from being pulled apart or moved in the wrong direction.

Knee joint

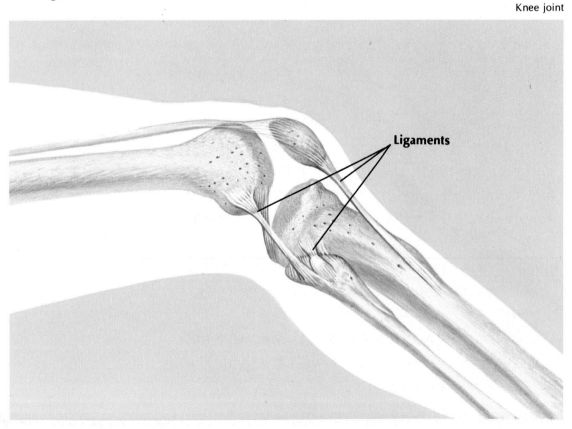

Ligaments

Here's a way to have a closer look at some joints. You will need an uncooked whole chicken leg and a pair of heavy scissors.

Take the meat off the bone. Find the joint and bend it back and forth. What kind of joint is it? Look at the ends of the bones. Find the ligaments that hold the bones together at the joint. Try to break the ligaments by bending the joint sideways or backward. How strong are they?

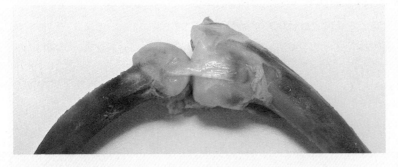

Carefully cut away the ligaments on one side. How are the ends of the bones shaped? Feel the smooth cartilage at the end of the bones. Notice that the cartilage is very slippery. It is covered with an oily liquid. Why is this oily liquid important?

Have your teacher saw one of the bones open. Find the marrow in the middle. Why do you think it is red?

Look at the picture of a person's knee joint. Compare the chicken bones with those in the picture. How are they alike?

How Do Bones Move?

Your bones do not move by themselves at the joints. Your bones support you as you move, but it is the **muscles** [MUHS-uhlz] attached to them that move bones. You have more than 600 muscles, big and small. You have muscles in almost every part of your body. You can blink your eyes and wiggle your nose. You can kick a ball and smile because you have muscles that can do these things.

How are children using muscles in this photo?

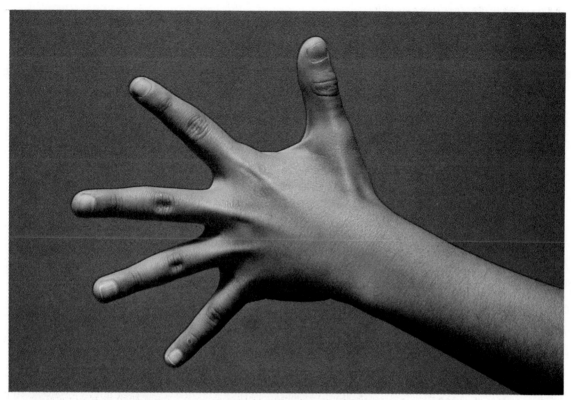

Can you see the tendons?

Look at the back of your hand. Open and close your hand a few times. Do you see the long cords just under the skin? These are called **tendons** [TEHN-duhnz]. Tendons attach the muscles in your hand to the bones. Touch the tendons as you open and close your hand. Do they feel strong and stringlike?

Most muscles work in pairs. One muscle lowers your arm and another muscle lifts it. You have several pairs of muscles in each arm. You have other pairs of muscles in your legs, fingers, and toes. When one muscle in the pair pulls, the other one rests. Almost all your movements are made by muscles working in pairs.

Let's see how a pair of muscles make a part of you move.

Let one arm hang loose. Feel the long muscle that goes from your shoulder almost down to your elbow. Now lift just the lower part of your arm slowly. Do you feel the muscle getting shorter and thicker?

Lower this part of your arm and feel the muscle become longer and thinner again. Move your arm up and down a few more times. As you do this, feel the changing shape of your muscle. Notice that the muscle is thicker in the middle and becomes thinner toward each end. Perhaps you can feel the thin, hard tendon at each end.

You have just felt the lifting member of the pair of muscles in your arm. Here is a way to feel the other member—the muscle that lowers your arm.

Rest your arm on your desk with the inside of your hand facing you. With the other hand, feel the long muscle in the back of your upper arm.

Now push down on the desk. Feel the muscle in your upper arm become hard. This is the muscle that pulls the lower part of your arm down.

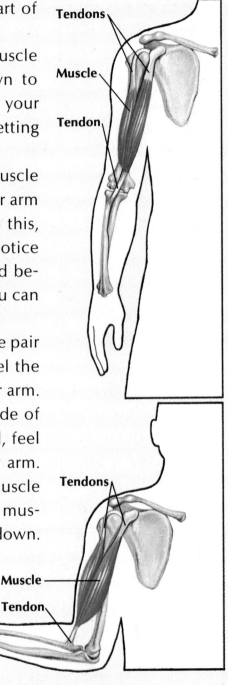

Tendons

Muscle

Tendon

Tendons

Muscle

Tendon

What motion can you make with your arm, leg, or other part of your body? On the picture, try to find the muscle that causes the motion. Make this motion, touching your muscle as you do so. How can you tell whether you are touching the right muscle?

From head to foot, every move you make is made by your muscles. Healthy muscles are firm and springy. They give your body a good shape and form. Your muscles will get firmer and stronger if you exercise properly every day.

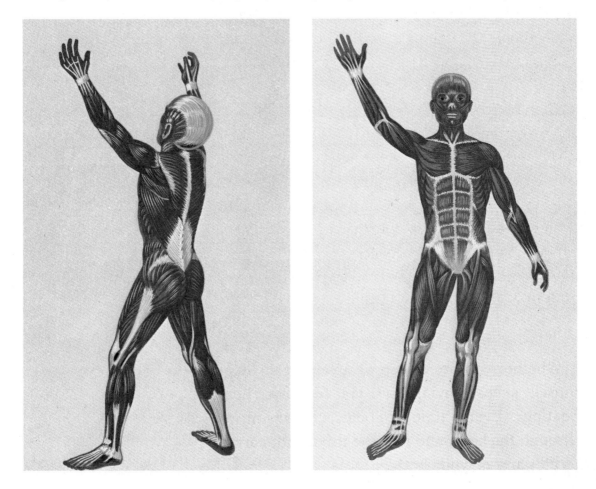

Muscles That Move on Their Own

When you kick a ball, ride a bicycle, or write a letter, you are moving muscles. These muscles move because you want to move them. But you have other muscles that move whether you want them to or not.

The muscles in your stomach and intestines move even though you may not know it. When there is food in the stomach or intestines, muscles move without your thinking about it.

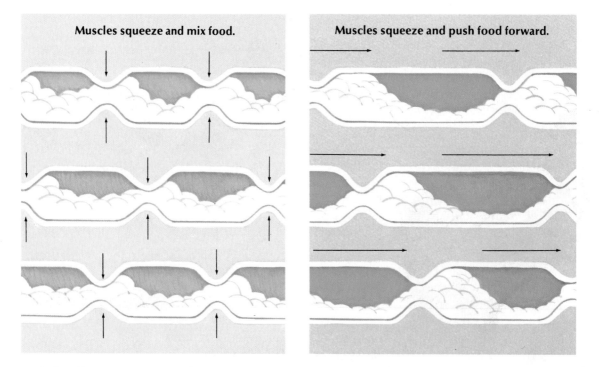

Muscles squeeze and mix food.

Muscles squeeze and push food forward.

Whether you are asleep or awake, your heart muscle keeps moving. Can you feel your heart beating? Every time it beats, blood moves through the heart and into the tubes that carry it to all parts of your body.

Here's a way to find out how many times your heart muscle moves in one minute.

Lay your left arm on your desk, with the inside of your hand facing you. Place the first two fingers of your right hand on the inside of your left wrist. Press lightly with your fingers. What you feel is the blood pushing against the muscles of your blood tubes. This is called your pulse, and it is caused by the beating of your heart muscle.

Take your pulse for one minute. How many times did your heart muscle move? Now, without moving, try to make your heart muscle beat faster. Can you do it by just thinking about it?

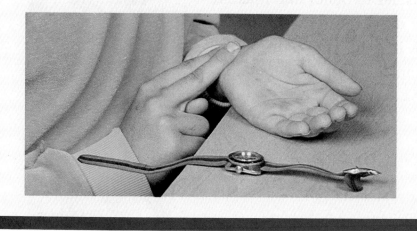

There are muscles in your throat and eyelids that move on their own, too. Once you have swallowed milk, can you stop it from passing into your stomach? If you look in a mirror, can you stop the muscles in your eyelids from blinking? Find out at home tonight.

What Did You Learn?

- A skeleton is made of bones that support and protect the body.
- Bones have minerals in them that make them hard and strong.
- Parts of your blood are made in the bone marrow.
- A joint is the place where two bones are joined together by ligaments to allow movement.
- Cartilage lets the bones move more easily and keeps them from rubbing against one another.
- Tendons attach muscles to bones and make it possible for you to move.
- Most muscles work in pairs; one pulls in one direction and one in the opposite direction.
- Some muscles move whether you want them to or not.

Biography

Maggie Lettvin (1927–   )

Bones and muscles are part of "the beautiful machine." "The beautiful machine" is how Maggie Lettvin, author and television star, describes your body.

Maggie Lettvin was in an automobile accident that caused pain down her shoulders and arms. Through reading many books, she found exercises that would free her of the pain. After doing them, she found that she felt better than ever before!

She began teaching her exercises on television and radio shows. She has also taught courses and written books on how to stay fit.

Many people, from homemakers to office workers and from children to old people, write to Maggie Lettvin. She teaches these people how to improve their bodies through exercise.

TO THINK ABOUT AND DO

On a piece of paper copy the sentence clues. Next to each clue, name the part of your body or the material that is being described. Choose your answers from the list of words.

1. They join two bones together at joints.
2. It keeps the bones from rubbing against each other.
3. They attach muscles to bones.
4. When you move, it supports and protects your body.
5. They work in pairs, but move in opposite directions.
6. They make bones hard and strong.
7. This part of the bone makes parts of your blood.

cartilage

muscles

tendons

minerals

skeleton

ligaments

marrow

What kinds of joints are found in these parts of your body? Write the letters a through g on a piece of paper. Next to each letter, write the name of the joint.

These charts give average heights for boys and girls. Use your weight and age to find where you are on the chart. Figure out how tall you will be at 12, 14, and 16.

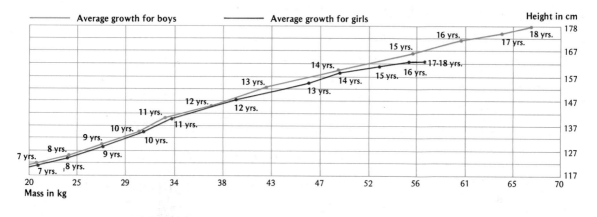

— Average growth for boys ——— Average growth for girls

Height in cm

Mass in kg

ACTIVITY

Some muscles move whether you want them to or not. To see how one of these muscles works, you will need a large bowl of water. Ask a friend to help you.

Make a fist with one of your hands. Your fist is about the size of your heart. Put your fist under the water and squeeze it in and out. Watch the water squirt out between your thumb and forefinger.

Now ask your friend to time you as you squeeze in and out as fast as you can. How many times can you do this in a minute? How long can you do this before becoming tired? Fortunately for you, your heart muscle pumps blood in and out without tiring.

Structures Explain the Behavior of Matter

4

Matter

The world is so full of objects! There are soft objects—powder, flower petals, air; and there are hard objects—rocks, seashells, ice. There are bright objects—stars, fireflies, flames; and there are dull objects—dust, tree bark, smoke.

Sweet, sour, smooth, rough, wet, dry, hot, cold! Shut your eyes a moment and think of all the words that tell about the objects around you! Then try to think of all the kinds of objects these words could be used with.

Look around you! How many different objects can you name in two minutes? The world is so full of objects, and yet they are all alike in one way. They are all made of **matter** [MAT-uhr]. In fact, everything in the world is made of matter.

photo at left: Everything in the picture is made of matter.

What Is Matter?

Try to find something that does not take up any room. Is it possible to do this? Here is a glass full of milk. Do you think it can hold any more?

Can you put more toys in this box?

What happens if you add too much air to this balloon? What does this tell you about the air in the balloon?

The milk, the toys, and the air all take up space. There is a certain amount of matter present in the space that each of these things takes up. The amount of matter in each thing, or in anything else you can name, is its **mass** [mas].

112

Here is a way to show that matter takes up space. You will need a glass, a bowl, and some water.

Put the glass in the bowl. Fill the glass with water. Now find an object that will fit into the glass. What do you think will happen when you carefully put it into the glass of water? Try it and see if you are right. Try to put some other objects into the water. Does the same thing happen with each one? What does this tell you about matter?

What happens when you throw a ball up into the air? The ball, water, and diver fall down. Can you throw the ball so high that it won't come back?

The earth pulls down on all matter with a force that you cannot see. This downward pull or force is called **gravitation** [grav-uh-TAY-shuhn]. The earth's gravitation never stops pulling on objects. Its pull even keeps you from falling off the earth!

Waterfall

Diver

Although you cannot see gravitation, you know it is there. Every time you try to lift something, you are lifting the object against this force. The more mass an object has, the greater is the force of gravitation on that object. Which has the greater mass, the books that are tied together or the book that is alone? Which do you think will take the greater force to lift?

Measuring the force of gravitation

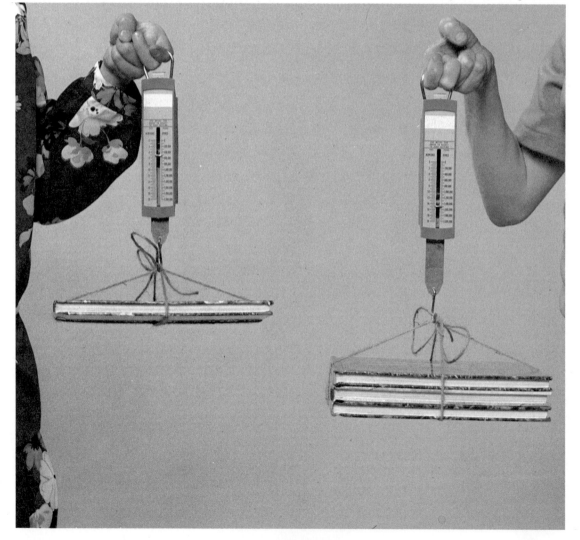

Tiny Particles of Matter

Now you have learned three things about matter. You know that all matter has mass and takes up space. You also know that the earth's gravitation pulls down on all matter. But all matter is alike in still another way! It is made of particles too tiny to see.

Think of the pile of sand that you can see across the street. You can see the whole pile, but you cannot see the separate grains. As you come closer, you begin to see the little grains of sand. Think about how many grains of sand there must be in the pile.

Grains of sand

Each grain of sand is made of many, many smaller particles. They are so small that you cannot see them. These tiny particles are called **atoms** [AT-uhmz].

How many atoms are there in each grain? There are more atoms in one grain of sand than there are leaves on all the trees in the world! It is very hard to imagine anything so tiny.

Here is a way to find out more about matter. You will need some salt, a hand lens, a paper cup, several toothpicks, and some water. Also get a piece of dark paper, a saucepan, a hammer, a pin, a spoon, a source of heat, and safety glasses.

Put a few grains of salt on a piece of dark paper. Look at them with your hand lens. What shapes are the salt grains? How big do they look through the lens?

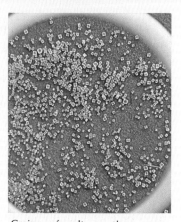

Grains of salt as they appear through a hand lens

Cover the salt with a piece of paper. Crush the salt by tapping it lightly with a hammer or some other hard object. Now what is the shape and size of the salt grains? How do you think you could separate them into still smaller pieces?

Stir a spoonful of salt into a paper cup almost full of water. Can you see the salt now? With a clean toothpick, take one drop of water from the top. Taste it. Is there salt in the water at the top?

Make a pinhole in the middle of the paper cup. Touch another toothpick to the drop that comes out. Is there salt in the middle of the water? Taste the water from a pinhole at the bottom. Is there salt at the bottom of the water? Is there any place where there is no salt? How can you tell?

You can't see the salt, but you can taste it in all parts of the water. This could not happen if salt were not made of very tiny pieces. You can't see these tiny pieces with the hand lens, but you can prove they are there.

Pour the water into a pan and heat it until the water is gone. What is left in the pan?

Studying different kinds of matter

All matter is made of atoms. But you can't see any atoms when you look at your smooth desk. You can't see the atoms in rocks, plants, or animals, either. But they are there! Different kinds of atoms make up all the different kinds of matter in the world.

It's hard enough to believe that matter is made of atoms too small to be seen. Here's something even harder to believe: Each atom is always moving and is moving very fast, at that!

Look at your hand, your fingernail, and the page of this book. Everything you see is made of separate, moving atoms. The atoms are so small and move so fast that you cannot feel their motion.

Copper wire

Iron nail

Iron pan

Silver necklace

Water drop

All the matter on the earth is made of about 90 different kinds of atoms. This piece of wire, for example, is made of moving atoms of copper. This nail is made of iron atoms and so is this pan. There is only one kind of atom that makes up this necklace. Can you tell what atoms are moving in the necklace?

Sometimes atoms come together in a certain way. They may be the same kinds of atoms, or they may be different. When atoms come together in this way, they form a **molecule** [MAHL-uh-kyool] of matter. For example, **hydrogen** [HY-druh-juhn] atoms and **oxygen** [AHK-suh-juhn] atoms may come together in a certain way. These two kinds of atoms may form a molecule of water. In one drop of water there are hundreds of billions of these moving water molecules.

Ice cube

Matter That Keeps Its Shape

The water in this ice cube is frozen. If you could look inside the ice cube, you would see that the water molecules are packed very closely together. The water in this cube is in a form called a **solid** [SAHL-ihd]. In a solid such as ice, each molecule is rapidly shaking back and forth. A pull or force holds each molecule to the ones around it, even though each molecule is moving back and forth.

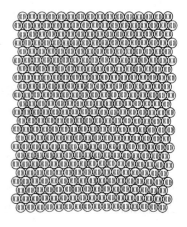

Molecules of a solid move rapidly in place.

120

Look at the ruler. Suppose you could mark a certain molecule near one end and another in the middle. If you looked at the ruler in 30 minutes, would you find the molecules in the same place? Based on what you learned about molecules in a solid, you should.

Can you see the numbers on the ruler move?

A clump of molecules has already been marked for you. Look at the clump of molecules in the shape of a number 1. Do you think it will be there in 30 minutes? Or will these molecules spread around and move among the other molecules of the wood? Look at this ruler again after 30 minutes. Does this help you believe that the molecules of a solid hold their place?

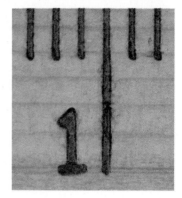

Matter That Does Not Keep Its Shape

When a solid such as ice is heated, its molecules begin to move faster. As the molecules move faster, they roll and slide over and around each other. The more heat that is added, the faster the molecules move. When the molecules begin moving really fast, they can more easily overcome the force or pull between them. Finally, the force is not strong enough to hold the molecules in place. The ice melts. The water is changed from a solid to another form called a **liquid** [LIHK-wihd].

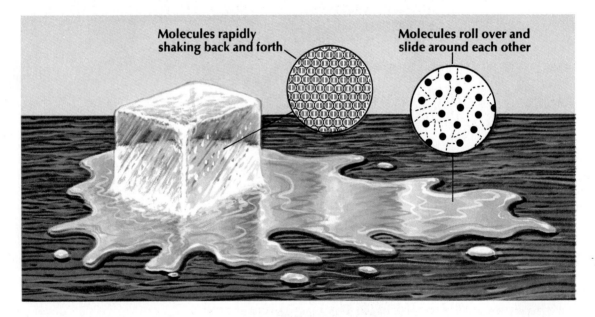

Molecules rapidly shaking back and forth

Molecules roll over and slide around each other

The water molecules in a liquid and in a solid are the same. But there is one difference. The liquid water does not have a shape of its own. It just flows until it fits the shape of the solid that holds it—a cup, a bottle, or the floor.

Will adding heat to a solid change it in some way? Your teacher will give you a clear bag with an ice cube in it.

See if you can melt your ice cube faster than anyone else. Your teacher will tell you when to start. You can do anything to the ice cube to melt it. Remember to save the water from the ice cube. This is proof that you melted it. How long did it take your ice cube to change to water? Where did the heat energy come from that helped change the solid?

If you could mark a single water molecule and watch it, what would you see? Would you find it in the same place 30 minutes from now? A molecule of a liquid never stays in the same place. It moves around and also shakes back and forth and from side to side.

You can see what happens when molecules of a liquid bump into molecules of a solid. You will need a tablet of food coloring and a glass of water. Also get some crayons, some paper, and a watch or clock.

Drop the tablet of food coloring into the water. Don't touch or shake the glass or the water. Carefully watch what happens.

Use your crayons to make a drawing of what you see. Do this every three minutes. What are the molecules of water doing to the molecules of food coloring? Think about how the color spreads through the water, even without your stirring it.

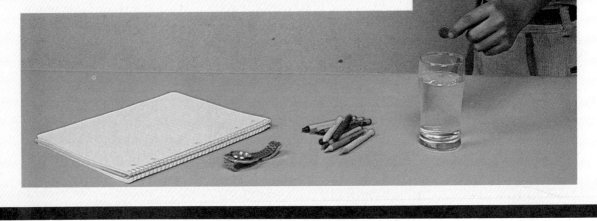

If you drop a tablet of food coloring into a glass of water, you will see the color spread through it. The water molecules will bump into the molecules of the tablet. Molecule by molecule, the food coloring will be moved around by the moving molecules of water.

Matter That Can Fill Any Space

You have seen that heat energy can change matter from a solid to a liquid. You know, for example, that heat energy will cause frozen water to become liquid water. What happens if you add still more heat energy?

You know that molecules in a liquid are moving all the time. They move in all directions, bumping into each other and bouncing away. Sometimes a molecule at the top of a liquid may get bumped upward by a molecule below it. The bump may have just enough force to throw it out of the water. Now the molecule is no longer part of the liquid. It is a separate molecule of gas in the air. This gas is called water vapor. Whenever a liquid changes to a gas, we say that **evaporation** [ih-vap-uh-RAY-shuhn] takes place.

During evaporation liquid molecules change to gaseous molecules.

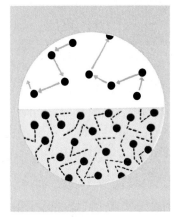

125

Here is a way to find out more about evaporation. You will need three containers: two flat pans of the same size and a bottle. Also get a measuring cup, some water, and a cover that you can see through.

Put the same amount of water in each of three containers. Place the cover over one of the pans.

From which container will the water evaporate most quickly? Why do you think so? See if you are right. Let the containers stand, and watch them every day for five days. How will you know which one lost the most water by evaporation?

Although evaporation may take place at any temperature, it can be speeded up by adding heat energy. You have seen this happen many times. When liquid water is heated, its molecules begin to move faster and faster. When this water becomes hot enough, bubbles of gas are formed. These bubbles move rapidly to the top and pop out of the liquid.

Boiling water

Gas molecules bump into each other, bounce off, and fly away in every direction. Since the gas molecules are moving so quickly, large empty spaces form between them. The force or pull between these molecules is too weak to hold them together. How are molecules in liquids and solids different from molecules in gases?

How do gas molecules move? To help you find out, your teacher will have two small bottles of perfume. Your teacher will put one bottle in an open shoe box, take off the bottle top, and quickly close the lid on the shoe box. Your teacher will then open the other bottle of perfume and leave it on a desk in front of the room.

When you smell the perfume, raise your hand. Why doesn't everyone smell the perfume at the same time?

Now open the shoe box and smell. Almost as many molecules came from the perfume bottle in the box as from the other bottle. But why does the perfume in the box smell stronger?

Some of the perfume molecules spread out between the moving molecules of air. The perfume molecules were shaken and bumped around. Bit by bit they were pushed farther and farther among the air molecules. When they reached your nose, you smelled the perfume.

Odors travel through the air.

Perhaps you never thought of odors as real things, but they are! When you pass the door of a bakery you smell many good things. When there is something good cooking in the kitchen, you can smell it all over the house! You are really smelling molecules of gas scattering through the air. Can you think why you can't smell old cake as easily as cake that is fresh from the oven? Why do you think a window is opened to help get rid of odors in a room?

Heat Energy and Solids, Liquids, and Gases

Look at this hand. It's a solid that you can see easily. The water in the glass is a liquid; you can see it too. But all around the hand and the water there is air. Why can't you see it?

To help you answer this question, look at these two groups of dots. The dots in "A" stand for molecules in a liquid. The dots in "B" stand for a gas. There are the same number of molecules in each group. But the molecules are much farther apart in one form of matter than in the other.

Comparing molecules in a liquid (A) and a gas (B)

Put this book on a desk or shelf, with this page open. Look at the two groups as you back away slowly. What happens as you move away from the book? Now can you tell why it's hard to see most gases? Why is it easier to see solids and liquids?

When you add heat energy to a solid, it may change to a liquid. When you heat a liquid, it may change to a gas. How would the motion of the molecules change if the solid were changed to a liquid? If the liquid were changed to a gas? But what happens to the motion of the molecules when you take heat energy away from a gas or a liquid?

What do you think will happen if you add heat energy to the molecules in any of these things? Will the spaces between the molecules change?

Solid, Liquid, or Gas?

These children went on a hunt. They brought to class many of the things they found. They decided to put them into three groups—solid, liquid, and gas.

Comparing solids, liquids, and gases

Would you be able to tell whether something is a solid, liquid, or gas? Here's a way to find out.

You will need five or six kinds of matter. They should include matter from all three groups—solid, liquid, and gas.

On a piece of paper, make three columns. Label them solid, liquid, and gas. For each object that you have chosen, decide whether it is a solid, a liquid, or a gas. Then write the name of that object in the correct column.

Here are some questions that may help you decide:

Does it have a shape of its own?

Does its shape stay the same when you squeeze it?

Can you pour it into a glass?

If you could heat it, would its shape be changed?

If you could cool it, how would it be changed?

Does it seem to belong in more than one column?

Solid	Liquid	Gas

When you have finished, check your list of objects with others. Keep adding to your list as you learn more about matter. Perhaps you had an orange or some noodle soup. Or maybe you brought a beach ball to class. In which columns should each of these be placed? Why did you need to place them in more than one column?

Using and Reusing Matter

People use very little of the world's matter exactly the way they find it. Most of the time people change matter in some way before they use it. They melt solids and they freeze liquids. They also evaporate liquids to change them to gases.

The kind of matter is not changed when people change its form. The only thing that is changed is how fast the molecules are moving. Since the form of matter can be changed, some kinds of matter can be used over and over again. Why is this so important in our world today?

Glass and metal are kinds of matter that can be used over and over again. Glass bottles, for example, are crushed, heated, and changed to liquid glass. The hot liquid glass is then used to make new bottles and other glass objects. Why should people collect and reuse matter? What difference would it make to you?

Recycling glass

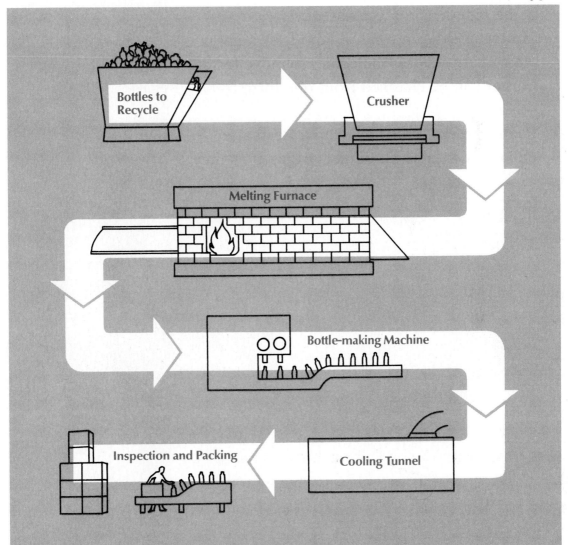

Bottles to Recycle

Crusher

Melting Furnace

Bottle-making Machine

Cooling Tunnel

Inspection and Packing

What Did You Learn?

- All matter takes up space and has mass.
- The earth pulls down on all matter with a force called gravitation.
- All matter is made of atoms that are rapidly moving.
- Molecules of matter are formed when atoms come together in a certain way.
- Matter is either a solid, a liquid, or a gas.
- Heat energy causes molecules to move faster.
- Matter can be changed from one form to another.
- People freeze, melt, or evaporate matter to change it to a solid, liquid, or gas that they can use.

Biography

Robert Brown (1773–1858)

How did people find out that molecules move by bumping into each other and bouncing back and forth? In 1827 Robert Brown, a person who studied plants, looked through a microscope and saw something strange.

Brown mixed water with a powder that flowers make. While he was looking at the powder, he noticed that its tiny grains were moving in many directions. He thought the grains were moving because they might be alive. However, he found that tiny bits of material that were not alive also moved in water. He couldn't explain why this happened, but he reported what he found out anyway.

Finally, in the 1860's, it was found out that water molecules were bumping into the grains. This bumping caused the grains to move in many directions.

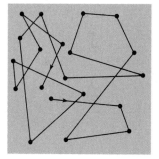

We now know that tiny bits of a solid always move in a liquid in this way. Robert Brown is important because he was the first person to see proof that molecules move.

TO THINK ABOUT AND DO

Copy and complete the sentence on a piece of paper.

1. Every kind of object that takes up space and has mass is _____.

2. Most objects fall toward the earth because of _____.

3. All matter is made of particles called _____ that are always moving.

4. When liquid molecules change to water vapor, we know that _____ has taken place.

5. Matter may be either a _____, a _____, or a _____.

WHAT DO YOU REMEMBER?

Each picture shows something being done to an object. In each case, the molecules of which the object is made move from one place to another. Write how you could tell that such movement has taken place in each picture.

138

1. Can you name one kind of matter that can be found as a solid, a liquid, or a gas?
2. Why does crushing a lump of sugar help it dissolve more rapidly?

WHERE DO THE ANIMALS BELONG?

These pictures stand for the way matter looks as a gas, a liquid, and a solid. What animal would you put in each picture? Tell why you chose each animal's habitat as you did.

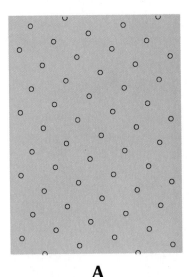

A

B

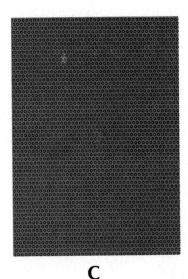

C

alligator	camel	canary
rabbit	goldfish	chipmunk
caterpillar	bat	catfish
dove	robin	eagle

The Earth's Atmosphere

5

Did you know that you live near the bottom of an ocean that is about 3000 km deep? Look all around you. You probably did not know you live here because the ocean is made of something you can't see. It is made of air!

The ocean of air covers the earth like a giant blanket. This blanket of air is called the **atmosphere** [AT-muhs-fihr]. The atmosphere is kept in place by the earth's gravitation. Air is as much a part of the earth as the land and the ocean. There would be no winds, water, clouds, or sky if you were to take away the atmosphere. Each day the sun would heat the earth's surface hotter than boiling water. Each night the earth would be colder than ice. Without the atmosphere, there would be no life on the earth.

photo at left: View from the upper levels of Earth's atmosphere

141

The Air Around Us

Air is matter. What do you know about matter? Let's see if these things are also true of air.

Have you ever heard anyone say something was "as light as air"? What did this mean? Although air seems very light, it has some mass. From its mass, given in grams, we know how much air there is. In the picture, which basketball has more air? Which side of the balance appears to have the greater mass? What does this tell you about air?

Does air have mass?

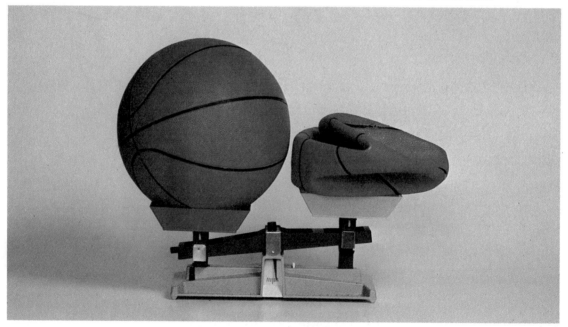

You have probably held a bottle under water and seen the bubbles of air coming from it. You noticed that water could not enter the bottle until some air had come out. Air was taking up space in the bottle.

Here's another way to show that air takes up space. You will need a funnel, a bottle, some clay, and some water.

Put the funnel into the bottle. Have someone hold the funnel down firmly while you pack clay around the funnel and the top of the bottle. You must make a good seal around the funnel with the clay.

What happens when you pour water into the funnel? Why do you think this happened?

Each of these bottles is full of air. What is the shape of the air in each bottle? How do you know? Which bottle has the most air inside it? How can you tell?

Matter takes up space and has mass. Matter is either a solid, a liquid, or a gas. Which form of matter is air? Why do you think that?

What Is Air Made Of?

Air is really made up of many different gases. About four-fifths of the earth's atmosphere is **nitrogen** [NY-truh-juhn]. About one-fifth of it is oxygen. There are many other gases in the atmosphere. Two of these are **carbon dioxide** [KAHR-buhn dy-AHK-syd] and **water vapor** [WAW-tuhr VAY-puhr]. But these other gases make up only a small part of the atmosphere.

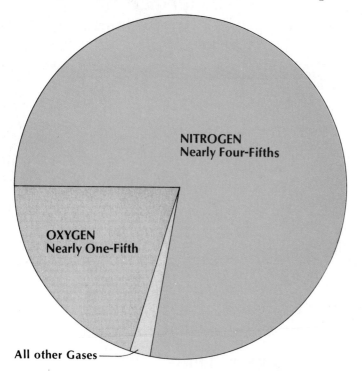

NITROGEN
Nearly Four-Fifths

OXYGEN
Nearly One-Fifth

All other Gases

Gases in the atmosphere

Oxygen is the most important gas for us. Every time you breathe in, oxygen goes into your body. The oxygen then combines with the food that you have eaten. In this way you get the energy that is stored in the food. Without oxygen you can't get energy from this food.

Let's see how we use oxygen to get energy. You will need a candle, a pan, several matches, some clay, a jar, and safety glasses.

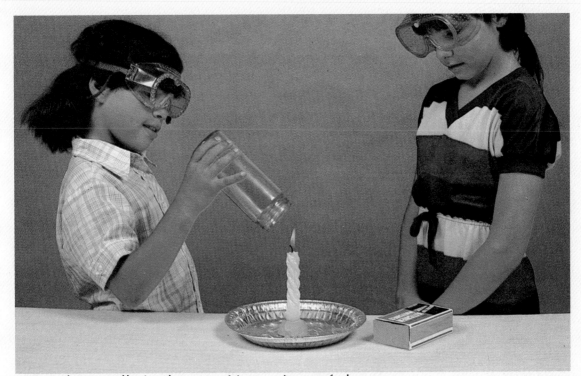

Put the candle in the pan. Use a piece of clay as a candleholder. Light the candle very carefully. What kinds of energy are being given off by the flame? Now, put the jar over the burning candle. What happens to the flame? Why can't the candle keep making light and heat energy? Without oxygen, the candle cannot give off light and heat energy. If the molecules of food that you have eaten do not get oxygen, your body cannot get energy from them.

Do you think that the air you breathe in is the same as the air you breathe out? Your body takes some oxygen out of the air that you breathe in. It puts some carbon dioxide into the air that you breathe out.

Since the air you breathe out has more carbon dioxide in it, you may not think it is very important for life. But there would be no life on Earth without carbon dioxide. Green plants take in the carbon dioxide that you breathe into the air. They use this gas, together with other materials and sunlight, to make food and to give off oxygen. Are you able to make food? Why couldn't you stay alive if there were no green plants?

You can test your own breath for carbon dioxide. You will need a liquid called limewater that tests for carbon dioxide, safety glasses, a straw, and a glass. Limewater turns a milky-white color when carbon dioxide is present in it.

Pour some limewater into a glass. Blow through a straw into the liquid for several minutes. What happens to the liquid? What does this tell you about the air that you breathe out?

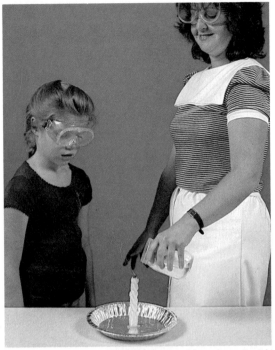

Experimenting with carbon dioxide

Carbon dioxide has another important use. This jar has vinegar and baking soda in it. The small circles you see rising in the liquid are bubbles of carbon dioxide. Look at what happens when some of the carbon dioxide gas is poured over a burning candle. What would be a good use for carbon dioxide?

Air also has water vapor in it. When water vapor cools, it may form clouds. As more water vapor cools within the cloud, it may change into rain, sleet, or snow. Why is water vapor an important part of the atmosphere?

There are small amounts of many other gases in the atmosphere. Together with nitrogen, oxygen, carbon dioxide, and water vapor, they make up the atmosphere that is around the earth.

Carbon dioxide extinguisher

Air Presses in All Directions

Each of the gases in the air takes up space and has mass. How much mass does air really have? How hard does its mass press on us each day?

What happens to the balls at the bottom of the box?

Each of these cotton balls is being pulled down by the earth's gravitation. Gravitation causes each ball to press down on the balls below it. The more a ball is pressed down, the more it presses against the balls around and beneath it.

Like the cotton balls, molecules of air have mass, too. Each air molecule presses down on the ones below it. Which air molecules have the most force pressing down on them? The force that causes air molecules to press against each other and everything around them is **air pressure** [ehr PREHSH-uhr].

Air pressure is all around you.

If you could find the mass of all the air above this boy, how much would it be? The mass of the air would be over 1000 kg, which is as much as a small car! Why doesn't all this air crush the boy?

How does air pressure act on you? The mass of the air around you causes a pressure that pushes on you from every direction. You can't feel this pressure because the spaces inside your body are also filled with air. The air inside you presses outward with the same force as the air around you. The air pressure inside your body is about the same as the air pressure outside your body. In this way you keep your shape and are not crushed by the pressure.

Let's see what would happen if the pressure inside your body were different from the pressure outside. The teacher asked these girls to press against the empty can to try and bend it.

When they could not bend the can, the teacher said that she would try something different. First she put some water in the can. Then she heated it until the water boiled. After the water boiled, the can was mostly filled with water vapor.

Now the teacher carefully took the can from the heat. Quickly and tightly, she put the top on. As the water vapor cooled, it changed back to liquid water. The liquid water took up much less space than the water vapor. This is because there was much less space between the molecules in the liquid. What happened to the can? Was the air pressure greater on the inside or outside of the can?

Suppose you climbed to the top of a mountain. Where do you think air molecules would press against each other more, on the mountaintop or in the valley? Since we can't see air molecules, the cotton balls will be used in their place. Think of a cotton ball near the top of the pile. Where does the pile of cotton balls press down more, on a ball near the top or on one at the bottom? Where is the air pressure greater?

Where is the air pressure greater, at the top of the mountain or at the bottom?

Do you think you could feel a difference in air pressure on the mountaintop? Sometimes you do when the car in which you are riding is driven up a mountain very quickly. Since the air molecules are farther apart on the mountaintop, the air has slightly less pressure. In this case, the pressure inside your body is greater than the pressure outside. You may feel your ears "popping" and want to swallow. Swallowing is your body's way of balancing the pressure inside your body with the pressure outside.

Air Pressure at Work

Air is all around you, pressing in all directions. Air pressure is used in all kinds of moving jobs. You can make something move by taking away air from one side. The air on the other side then pushes the object.

That is how a vacuum cleaner picks up dust. There is air all around the dust, pushing in every direction. If you take away air from one side, the dust will be pushed by air from the other side.

In a vacuum cleaner an electric fan keeps blowing air out of the cleaner. This leaves a space with fewer air molecules in a bag inside the cleaner. Outside air rushes into the space, pushing the dust along with it into the bag. The bag is made of cloth or of paper with tiny spaces in it. Air molecules can pass through these tiny spaces, but the dust cannot get through. The dust stays in the bag until the bag is emptied.

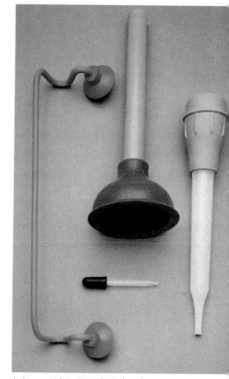

left to right: Towel rack, plunger, eyedropper, food baster

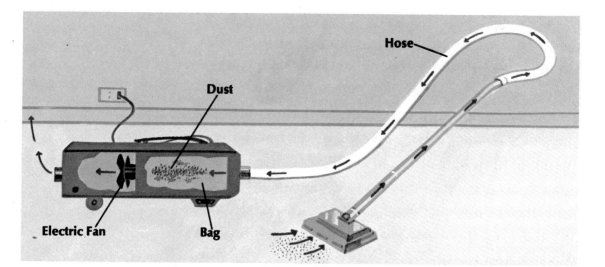

Hose

Dust

Electric Fan

Bag

How does air pressure move something? To find out, you will need a strip of paper about 12 cm long and 2 cm wide.

Hold the strip of paper in front of your lips. You know there are air molecules on both sides of the paper. If you take away some air molecules from one side, what will the air molecules on the other side do to the paper?

Draw some air into your mouth. What happens to the paper?

When you drink through a straw, how does the liquid move up the straw and into your mouth? First, you must suck some air molecules from the straw into your mouth. When you do this, air pressure becomes less inside the straw. What happens to the air pressure on the outside of the straw? Air pressure on the outside of the straw is now greater and pushes the liquid into the straw. What do you have to do to keep liquid moving up the straw?

Large arrows stand for increased air pressure; small arrows stand for reduced air pressure.

Pushing Air into a Small Space

Air that has been pressed into a smaller space is called **compressed air** [kuhm-PREHST ehr]. Since compressed air has more pressure than the air around it, it pushes outward with much greater force. People use compressed air in all kinds of ways, from breaking rocks to stopping a train or bus. How does changing the air pressure inside these things make work easier?

Uses of compressed air

Can you blow hard enough to lift a heavy book? Here is a way to find out. You will need some books and a large balloon.

Place a book on the balloon and blow air into it. What happens? Now try it with two books. See how many books you can lift with your breath. What happened to the air molecules that you blew into the balloon? Why were you able to lift the heavy books?

The pressure of the air in the atmosphere is changing all the time. Let's look at some of the reasons this can happen.

These two boxes are filled with the same number of molecules. But one box has only dry air molecules in it. The **moist** [moyst] air in the other box has molecules of water vapor among the dry air molecules. Which box has the greater mass, dry air or moist air?

The amount of water vapor in the air is not always the same. It changes from day to day and from place to place. Whenever there is more water vapor, the air has less mass. When the air is dry, it has greater mass. Which air molecules would press on a surface with greater force, dry air molecules or molecules with water vapor?

Cooling the air changes the amount of space the molecules move around in. When heat is taken away, more molecules can be packed into the same space. If there are more air molecules in the space, what happens to the air's mass?

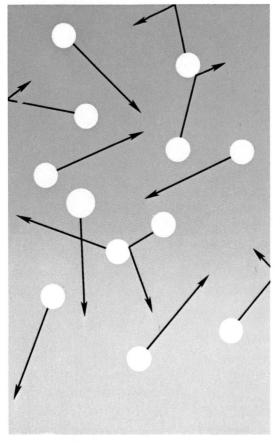

Warm air molecules

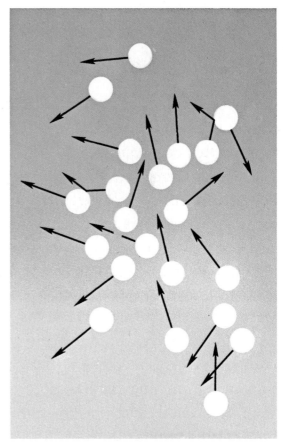

Cool air molecules

157

For example, cool air rushes out at you when you open a refrigerator door on a hot day. If you were dressed like the girl in this picture, what part of your body would feel the coldest? If this cool air has a greater mass, there must be more molecules pressing on the floor. You can see, then, that the air pressure of molecules of cool air is also greater.

Here is a way to see how air pressure can change. You will need two jars with covers and three pieces of string. Also get two paper clips, two paper bags, and a meterstick.

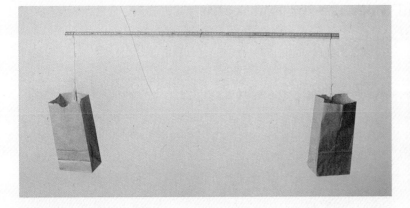

Take the top off one of the jars and leave it in a very cold place. Place the other jar in the room. Tie one end of a piece of string around the middle of a meterstick. Tie the other two pieces of string to each end of the meterstick. Hang a paper clip from the free end of each of these strings. Put open paper bags on each paper clip. Now, get everything to balance.

Put the top on the jar that is in the room. Bring it near one of the open bags. Take the top off the jar and tip it over the bag. What happens to the balance? Now, put the top on the jar that is in the cold place. Bring it near one of the open bags and take off the top. Tip the jar over the bag. What happens this time? What made the difference?

Heating Land and Water

Do you like to go swimming on a hot, sunny day? You know how cool and pleasant the water feels. The land is so hot and the water is so cool! But the same hot sun that shines on the water also shines on the land. Does the sunlight really warm the land more than the water? Or does it only feel that way?

Why is it often cooler at the seashore?

The temperature of the water in the ocean and in lakes does not rise as quickly as the temperature of the land. Since the water is cooler than the land, it helps to keep the air above it cool. Even if you don't go into the water, you usually feel cool near the water. This is because air over cool water is cooler than air over hot land. Some cool air over the water moves to the land where you are, and you get cooled.

How is this girl being cooled?

160

You can show that the temperature of the land rises faster than that of water because of the sun's energy. You will need two bowls, two thermometers, some water, and some dry soil. The water and soil should be at room temperature.

Fill one bowl half full of soil and the other half full of water. Put each thermometer just below the surface of the soil and the water. Write the temperatures on a piece of paper.

Put both bowls in a sunny place for ten minutes. Take the temperatures again and write them on your paper. Which bowl warmed up more in the sunlight?

Cooling Land and Water

What happens at night, after the sun goes down? At night, everything begins to cool off. But which cools off faster, the land or the water?

Have you ever gone walking along the shore on a summer night? As you stepped from the cool beach into the water, you found a surprise. The water was warmer than you expected! It had cooled off only a little bit after sunset, while the sand had cooled off much more.

Which foot will feel cooler?

Let's show that land cools off faster than water. You will need two bowls, water, dry soil, two thermometers, and a measuring cup.

Put one cup of dry soil into one bowl and one cup of water into the other bowl. Put both bowls in a warm, shady place. Leave them in this place until the soil and the water are at the same temperature. Use a thermometer to measure the temperatures and write these temperatures on a piece of paper.

Now you are ready to find out which kind of matter, soil or water, cools off faster at night. Put both bowls in a cool place for fifteen minutes. With the thermometers, measure the temperatures at the top of the soil and the water. Write these temperatures on your paper. Why does the soil have a lower temperature than the water?

Heating the Atmosphere

You know that the sun warms the land and water. But did you know that the sun warms the atmosphere very little? The atmosphere is made up of gases that do not become much warmer when sunlight passes through.

Yet you know that the air around you gets warm somehow. You can feel it, and you can also see the change it makes on a thermometer. Then how does the air get heated?

Sunlight heats the land and causes the molecules of the land to move more quickly. These heated molecules then move against the air molecules that are touching them. This makes the air molecules move faster. In this way, the air touching the ground is heated.

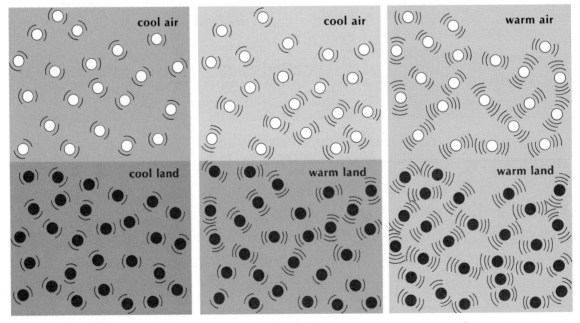

Night   Mid-morning   Afternoon

Glass, like the atmosphere, lets sunlight pass through it. Here's a way to see that glass does not get much warmer when light passes through it.

Put a sheet of black paper in the sun, near a closed window. After a few minutes, touch the paper. Does it feel warm? This is because the temperature of dark things rises quickly in the sun. Now touch the window glass. Does it feel warm? What is the difference between the glass and the black paper?

The sunlight that heated the black paper had to go through the glass first. Yet the sunlight heated the glass very little. In the same way, the sunlight that heats the land has to go through air first. But the sunlight does not heat the air as it goes through it. Instead, the sun heats the land molecules first. When the air molecules move against the land molecules, the air molecules get heated, too.

The flow of air in a heated room

Does it take more molecules of warm air than cool air to fill a certain space? Or does it take fewer? When warm and cool air meet, do they stay next to each other or do they move in some way? To find out, look at what happens when a radiator heats the air around it.

The radiator heats the air molecules that are closest to it. As these molecules get warmer, they begin to move more quickly and spread out. As the molecules spread out, there are fewer molecules in the space. The air becomes lighter and rises.

As the air rises, it loses heat and cools. The air molecules slow down and come closer to each other. Now there are more molecules in the same space. The air becomes heavier and sinks to the floor. When this heavier air reaches the radiator, the molecules get warmer, the air becomes lighter, and it rises once again.

Over and over, as air is heated and cooled, it moves around and around.

Here is a way to see how air moves. You will need a drinking straw and a piece of paper. With scissors cut the paper so that it is 8 cm wide and 10 cm long.

Now get a paper clip, a pencil, a pin, and some tape. Flatten one end of the straw. Tape a piece of paper to it. Push a pin through the middle of the straw and into the eraser of the pencil. Now flatten the other end of the straw. Slide a paper clip on this end. Make sure everything is balanced. You have made a tool that shows how air moves.

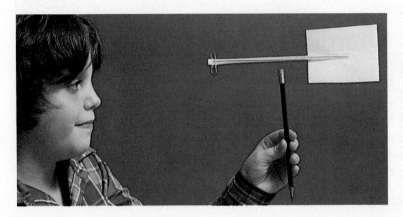

Hold the tool over a warm place. Which way does the paper move? What made the paper move? Which way does warm air move? Now, hold your tool below the bottom of a refrigerator door. Slowly open the door a few centimeters. Which way does the paper move? What made it move? Which way does cold air move?

Air on the Move

The winds outside your home are also made by the meeting of cool and warm air. At the beach on a sunny day, the air is warm and its molecules are far apart. Over the water, the air is cooler and its molecules are closer together. When this cooler air does spread out, some of it moves in toward the land. There it pushes its way under the warmer air.

Sea breeze

The cool air pushes the warm air up and out of the way. You feel a cool wind blowing from over the water across the warm land. This light wind is like what you felt coming from the open refrigerator door. This wind is called a sea breeze.

At night, the air over the land gets cool. But the air over the water does not cool as quickly. Where is the air heavier? Which way will the wind move? Draw a sketch on a piece of paper showing the way the wind will blow at night. This wind is called a land breeze.

Whether over land or water, you can find differences in the wind. Light winds move gently from the cool shade of a tree to the sunny fields. Or they may move from the shady side of a street to the sunny side.

What causes wind away from the seashore?

Cool air from the shady side of a mountain can also make a wind. It sweeps across a sunny valley where it takes the place of warmer, rising air. You can feel the wind when this happens.

Where the cool air is just a little cooler than the warm air next to it, the wind is gentle. The wind is strong where there is a big difference in the temperature of the warm air and the cool air. As you can see, wind is caused partly by unequal heating of the air.

Large temperature differences are one cause of wind.

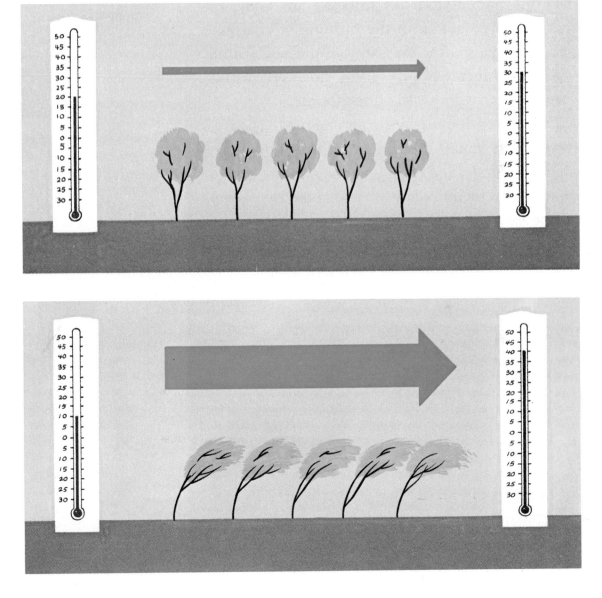

The Atmosphere: Today and Tomorrow

Living things need the ocean of air that is around them to stay alive. Therefore, we all must keep it as clean as we can.

But sometimes the air around us has matter in it that is harmful. Too much smoke and other harmful matter often get into the air. Some of this matter comes from the burning of coal, oil, and gas. The matter may stay in the air around where it is formed. Very often, however, winds spread it throughout the atmosphere.

The matter floating in the air can make it dirty. It can also make clothes, windows, buildings, plants, animals, and even you dirty. Many plants do not grow well in dirty air and some may even die because of it. The dirty air may make your eyes sting, itch, and water. If you breathe in air that is too dirty, you may even get sick.

Examples of air pollution

Factories and automobiles give off smoke and gases. The smoke and gases mix with water and oxygen in the air and form an **acid** [AS-ihd]. When the acid falls back to Earth in rain, it is called acid rain. Acid rain is harmful to plants, animals, and people. It can even damage statues and other stone or metal objects.

There are ways to stop harmful matter from getting into the air in the first place. People can clean the smoke that comes from buildings before it goes into the air. They can make cars run cleaner, too. Instead of driving cars, they can ride buses or use subways. They can find a clean way to get rid of trash instead of burning it.

What can you do to keep the air clean?

Ways to reduce air pollution

What Did You Learn?

- The earth's atmosphere is necessary for life.
- Air is matter because it has mass and takes up space.
- Air is made up of many different gases, including nitrogen, oxygen, carbon dioxide, and water vapor.
- Air pressure is caused by the force of air molecules pressing on a surface.
- Air pressure may change when the temperature and the amount of water in the air change.
- People use the differences in air pressure to help them do work.
- The sun heats the land, water, and air differently.
- When warm air meets cool air, it is pushed up by the moving, cool air.
- People can do many things to help keep harmful matter out of the air.

Career

Airplane Crew

The air around us is important in many ways. The movement of air can hold up a huge, heavy airplane. Airplanes have become a fast and safe way to travel.

If you have taken a trip in an airplane, you might have heard the pilot's voice over the loud-speaker. The pilot is in charge of the plane. The pilot and copilot use many instruments in the cockpit to make sure that the flight is safe and smooth.

Some flights have a person who is in charge of knowing where the plane is at all times. This person is the **navigator** [NAV-uh-gay-tuhr]. The navigator tells the pilot which route to follow and how long the flight will take.

The flight attendants are part of the cabin crew. They work to make the flight enjoyable for everyone. They help people get comfortable, serve food, and are trained to help passengers if any problems should arise.

There are many people who keep airplanes flying. Some of these workers build and repair airplanes. Others sell tickets, take care of baggage, and keep the airplanes safe in the sky.

TO THINK ABOUT AND DO

On a piece of paper copy the letters that make the word *atmosphere*. See how many science words you can make that begin with each letter. The letter "a" has been done for you.

a - air
t
m
o
s
p
h
e
r
e

Copy these sentences on a piece of paper. Choose the right word to finish the sentence.

1. There would be no life on earth without the _____.
2. The two gases that make up most of the atmosphere are _____ and _____.
3. The force of air molecules pressing on a surface is called _____ _____.
4. The sun's energy heats the _____ faster than the _____.
5. Air takes up space, has mass, and is made of tiny _____.
6. When warm air and cold air meet, a _____ is made.

nitrogen
molecules
wind
air pressure
atmosphere
oxygen
land
water

THE DART BOARD

Have you ever played this game? The person who gets the most darts in or near the center of the board wins the game. When you hit the board with the darts, the darts stay on the board. Why does this happen? In order to explain your answer, think about what happens in a vacuum cleaner or a soda straw.

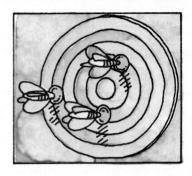

AIR ON THE MOVE

On a piece of paper write the answers to the following questions about what is happening in the picture.

Look at the arrows in this picture. In which direction is the air moving? Why is the air moving in this direction? Where would you rather be on a hot, sunny day—in the valley or in the mountains?

Structures Describe the
Solar System

Unit IV

The Solar System

6

If you have ever watched the stars, you may have noticed something interesting. Scattered among the stars in the night sky are several objects that are somewhat different. These objects don't appear to twinkle as the stars do. In fact, you couldn't see them at all if it weren't for the sun's light shining on them. They shine with a bright, steady light because they reflect light from the sun.

photo at left: The planets Jupiter, Saturn, and Mars as they appeared in July, 1982.

Objects in the Sky

To the ancients, these objects looked the same size as the stars that they appeared to wander among. Ancient people called each of these objects a wanderer or a **planet** [PLAN-iht]. But each planet is really much smaller than the sun or any other star. Can you think of a planet that you already know well?

Earth is a planet; so are **Mercury** [MUR-kyuh-ree], **Venus** [VEE-nuhs], and **Mars** [mahrz]. The surfaces of these planets are rocky. Together, they are called the inner planets because they are closest to the sun. Farther away are the planets **Jupiter** [JOO-puh-tuhr], **Saturn** [SAT-uhrn], **Uranus** [YUR-uh-nuhs], and **Neptune** [NEHP-toon]. They are much bigger, and some may be only mixtures of gases and liquids with no really solid surfaces. **Pluto** [PLOO-toh], the last planet, is now known to be mostly ice. Pluto is the farthest planet from the sun, except for those times when it passes inside Neptune's path.

Between the planets of Mars and Jupiter is a group of thousands of unevenly shaped objects—the **asteroids** [AS-tuh-roydz]. They range in size from Ceres, which is as large as Texas, to tiny pieces as small as dust. Some scientists think this dust was formed when the asteroids crashed into each other.

Mercury and Jupiter with moon

The solar system

All of these objects—the sun, the planets, and the asteroids—have something in common. They are members of a group, in much the same way that you, your classmates, and your teacher are members of a classroom group. In each of these groups, all members of the group act on the other members. But one member, the sun, for example, acts more strongly than the rest. Your teacher helps you and your friends to understand things and, in this sense, acts more strongly on all of you. Any group whose members act on each other and has one member that acts more strongly on the other members is one kind of **system** [SIHS-tuhm].

Example of a system

A baseball and a bat make a system. When the bat strikes the ball, the ball moves through the air. Actually, your arm muscles are part of this system, too. The strength of these muscles causes the bat to strike the ball with enough force to move it. Can you think of other examples of objects that belong to the system?

The sun, the planets, and the asteroids form a system, too. But this system has a special name. It is known as the **solar system** [SOH-luhr SIHS-tuhm]. What is it that keeps the members of the solar system together? You remember that all objects on the earth are acted on by the earth's gravitation. The sun also has this force of gravitation, but it is much stronger. Even though we cannot see this force, we know that it extends to all the parts of the system. In fact, it is the sun's gravitation that helps to hold the whole solar system together.

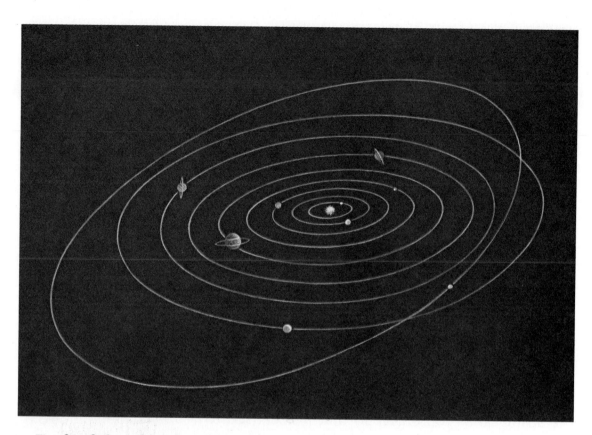

Each of the planets in the solar system moves in a path around the sun. Each of these paths is called an **orbit** [OHR-biht]. An orbit is shaped somewhat like the outline of a disk that you might draw on a piece of paper.

Objects that are already moving continue to move in a straight line unless a force acts on them. If the force of gravitation were not present, a ball that you threw into the air would keep going. In fact, it would never return to Earth. Since objects in motion tend to keep going in a straight line, why does each planet stay in its own orbit as it moves around the sun? Why doesn't a planet just fly into outer space?

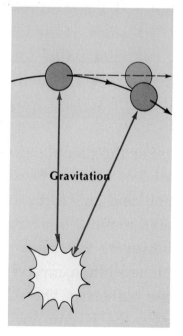

Gravitation

Here is a way to find out about how planets move around the sun. You will need a rubber eraser, a strong piece of string that is about 45 cm long, and safety glasses. Ask a friend to help you.

Tie one end of your string to the eraser. Hold the string by the other end and carefully whirl the eraser around. Ask your friend what kind of orbit the eraser follows as you whirl it. Is the orbit similar to the path taken by the planets?

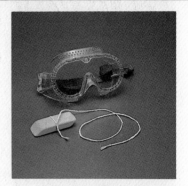

Again, whirl the eraser with your string. Do you feel the eraser pulling on the string? What do you think causes the pull? When you feel the pull on the string, you are really feeling the eraser moving away from its orbit. If it weren't for the string, the eraser would fly off in a straight line. Instead, the string holds the eraser so that it is caused to move in a curved path.

The sun's gravitation is like the string. The sun's gravitation holds the planets so that they are pulled into a curved path.

For the planets of the solar system, there is a kind of balance between flying off in a straight line and the force of gravitation. The planets tend to move in a straight line. At the same time, however, the sun's gravitation is pulling the planets into a curved path around it. In this way, the planets of the solar system can neither escape the system nor fall into the sun.

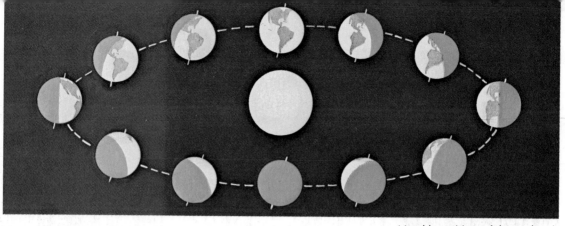

Monthly positions of the earth as it revolves around the sun

A Trip Around the Sun

If you are having a birthday today, it is an important day for you. But you will have to wait another year, the time it takes the earth to go around the sun, until your next birthday. The time it takes the earth to make one trip or **revolution** [rehv-uh-LOO-shuhn] around the sun is called a **year.** How many days are in an Earth year? How many times has the earth revolved around the sun since you were born? The chart shows how much time you would have to wait between birthdays if you lived on one of the other planets.

If you were in a great hurry and did not want to wait a long time between birthdays, what planet would you go to? Why would the time between birthdays be shorter on one planet than on another? A planet that is closer to the sun moves faster because it is under a stronger gravitational pull by the sun. Thus, the time it takes to make one revolution around the sun is shorter for the planet that is closer to the sun.

Planet	Period of Revolution in Earth Days and Years
Mercury	88 days
Venus	225 days
Earth	365¼ days
Mars	687 days
Jupiter	12 years
Saturn	29½ years
Uranus	84 years
Neptune	165 years
Pluto	248 years

Why do the planets take different lengths of time to make one revolution around the sun? Let's try something to find the answer. You will need a spool, a piece of string about a meter long, a clock, and a rubber eraser. Ask a friend to help you keep time.

Tie one end of the string to the eraser. Thread the other end through the hole in the spool. Then move the spool up the string. When you have done this, there should be about 20 cm left at the loose end of the string. Hold the spool in one hand. With your other hand, hold the loose end of the string under the spool.

Now whirl the eraser by moving the spool in a small circle. Keep your other hand still. Continue whirling the eraser as if it were a planet revolving around the sun. Do this until each revolution can be easily counted. Then have your friend record how many seconds it takes for the eraser to make five revolutions. Divide this number by five in order to find the number of seconds it takes to make one revolution.

Now pull the spool about 15 cm toward the loose end of the string. When you do this, what happens to the length of string between the spool and the eraser? Whirl the eraser as you did before and find the time it takes for one revolution. What does the time it takes the eraser to make one revolution around the spool have to do with its distance from the spool? What if the eraser were even farther from the spool? Would it take more time or less time for the eraser to make one revolution around the spool?

The Turning Earth

As each planet makes one revolution around the sun, it also spins like a giant top. Have you ever played with a top? You can make it spin or **rotate** [ROH-tayt] in one place. Nearly every 24 hours, the earth turns completely around or rotates. A **day** is the time it takes the earth to do this. On your ninth birthday the earth had rotated about 3300 times since the day you were born. That's a lot of spinning!

Earth spins like a giant top

Why do you think that you cannot feel the motion from all this spinning? The reason is that you cannot feel motion itself. You can only feel a speeding up or a slowing down. The changes in the earth's speed are so small and the time it takes the earth to rotate once is fairly long. For these reasons you do not notice any speeding up or slowing down.

190

How can you tell whether the earth's spinning affects you? To find the answer, you will need a globe, a light, clay, and a friend to help you.

Stick a small piece of clay on the state where you live. Shine the light on the globe. Have your friend slowly turn the globe. Can you tell when sunrise and sunset come to your state? When would you have noon and midnight?

The globe is a model of the earth. By shining the light on the globe as your friend rotates it, you can see how day and night follow each other.

But the earth's rotation every 24 hours does affect you. As the earth rotates, one side faces toward the sun and the other faces away from it. The side facing the sun is lighted by it; it is daytime on that side. The side away from the sun is in darkness; it is nighttime on that side.

Earth in light and darkness

Temperature and the Tilted Earth

For most places on Earth there is sunlight during some part of every day of the year. But the temperature of the air is not the same every day. Nor is the number of hours of sunlight the same every day of the year. A bright, sunny day in summer is usually much warmer than a bright, sunny day in winter. Everyone knows that the same sun shines on the earth at both times. What is it, then, that makes the difference?

In the summer, when you wake up early, the sun is already there, warming everything. In fact, you may get as many as sixteen hours of sunlight during the summer in some parts of this country. With so many hours of sunlight, the temperature can be quite high.

In winter, in the same place, you may get only eight hours of sunlight each day. The sun rises later and sets earlier. With fewer hours of sunlight, there is less time for everything to be warmed. The temperature of the air is usually lower. The number of hours of sunlight makes a difference in the temperature of the air.

How does the length of time when there is sunlight make a difference in the temperature of matter? To find out, you will need a thermometer, two bowls of the same size, a measuring cup, some water, and a clock.

Pour one cup of water into each bowl. Read and record the temperature of the water in each bowl. Then put one of the bowls in bright sunlight for 15 minutes. Be sure that the other bowl is not in the sunlight during this time.

After the 15 minutes has passed, put the other bowl in the sunlight for one minute. Then record the temperature of the water in each bowl. What difference did you find? What do you think made the difference?

The slant of the sun's rays also makes a difference in the temperature. During summer, the rays of the sun strike the earth's surface fairly directly. During winter, the sun's rays are more slanted when they strike the surface. In fact, the more the sun's rays are slanted on the area they cover, the less that area is heated.

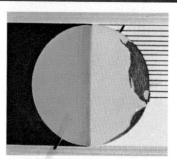

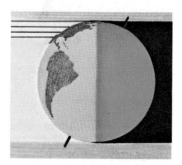

top: Direct rays of the sun during the summer in the Northern Hemisphere; *bottom:* Slanted rays of the sun during the winter in the Northern Hemisphere

What makes the difference between the temperature in summer and the temperature in winter? To find out, you will need a globe, some tape, a flashlight, and two white cards. Also ask a friend to help you.

Tape one of the cards to the **equator** [i-KWAY-tuhr], the band that goes around the middle of your globe. Tape the other card near the North Pole at the very top of your globe.

Shine a flashlight on the card at the equator. Look at the patch of light on the card. Does it look bright? How big is it? To find out, have your friend trace around the patch of light on the card.

Keeping the flashlight level and at the same distance from the globe as before, raise the light up until it shines on the card at the North Pole. Have your friend trace the patch of light on this card. Is this patch of light larger or smaller than the patch of light at the equator? Is it brighter or dimmer? Which part of the earth do you think would be warmed most by the light?

We now know that the slant of the sun's rays and the length of time the sun shines during one day can make a difference in the temperature that day. In the winter, for example, the sun's rays are more slanted and its energy is spread over a larger area. Because of these conditions and the fact that the sun shines fewer hours every day, the temperature of the air is lower in winter. But what is it that makes the sun's rays slant differently? Why does the sun shine a different length of time in winter than in summer?

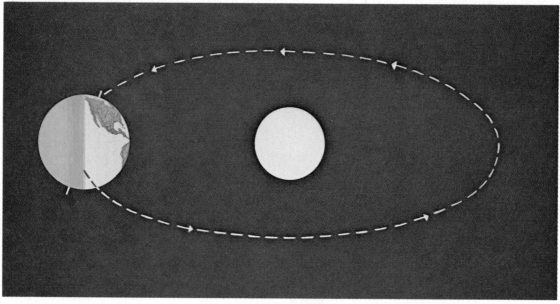

Summer in the Northern Hemisphere

On the first day of our summer, here is where the earth is in its orbit. Do you see how the North Pole is tilted *toward* the sun while the South Pole is tilted away? When the earth is in this part of its orbit, why do places north of the equator have warmer days than places south of the equator?

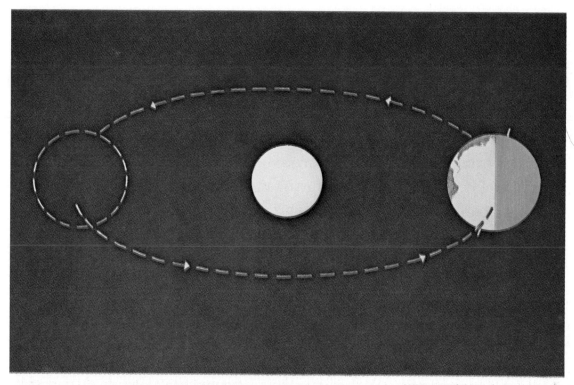

On the first day of our winter, the earth has traveled halfway in its orbit around the sun. Do you see how the North Pole is tilted *away* from the sun while the South Pole is tilted toward the sun? What difference does this make in the temperature where you live?

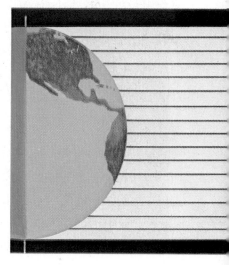

Winter in the Northern Hemisphere

Suppose the earth were not tilted at all as it moved. In this case, there would be twelve hours of sunlight and twelve hours of darkness each day. If there were no tilt, the sun's rays would strike the earth's surface at the same angle all year. If this happened, do you think there would be any temperature differences in different places on the earth? What would happen to the seasons that we have now?

There would be no seasons on the earth if the earth were not tilted. We know that the other planets are also tilted as they move around the sun. It is possible that some of them have seasons, too.

But the seasons on other planets are probably different from the seasons where you live. White caps have been seen on the north and south poles of Mars! They slowly shrink and disappear during the summer season at each pole. These caps are probably layers of frost or thin snow. Venus, on the other hand, rotates so slowly that a Venus day is 127 Earth days long. It would be hard to say that Venus has four seasons as we know them on Earth.

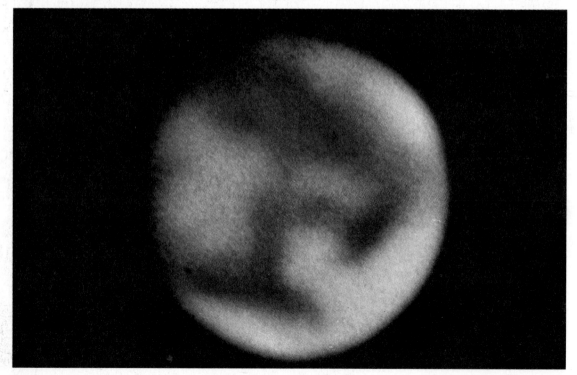

View of Mars with polar caps

Wandering Among the Stars

You remember that the planets puzzled the ancient star watchers. Even though the planets looked somewhat like the stars, they seemed different because of their changing positions in the sky. Not only did they seem to move among the stars; sometimes they seemed to go away altogether! Since all the planets revolve around the sun at different speeds, they appear at different places in the sky from month to month.

The changing position of Mars as it moves through its orbit

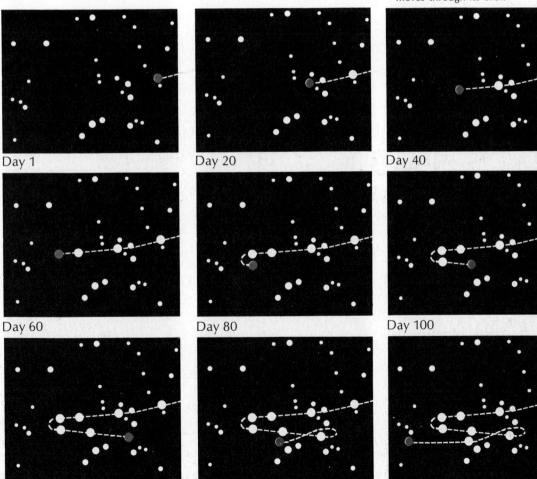

Day 1

Day 20

Day 40

Day 60

Day 80

Day 100

Day 120

Day 140

Day 160

199

Here is a way to understand why the planets' revolutions cause you to see them in different positions in the sky. Make four circles on the floor as in the picture. When the timekeeper claps his hands, Mars, on the outside circle, takes one step. In the next circle, Earth takes two steps. Do this several times, taking care that all the steps are the same size. See how Earth moves away from Mars. When does Earth begin moving near Mars?

To the next circle, add another planet, Venus. Venus should take three steps with each clap. Begin all three planets in a line. What happens as the planets circle the sun? Is there a time when Venus and Mars are both far from Earth? Is there a time when one is near and the other is far? When are both near?

Now add Mercury, the planet that is nearest the sun. Mercury must take four steps at every clap. Why is Mercury such a speedy planet?

Even though the planets of the solar system are much nearer than the stars, you cannot always see them. You cannot always point to the sky and say, "There is the planet Mercury. Near it is the planet Venus." Because of their different speeds, the planets sometimes look as if they are quite near each other and other times look as if they are farther apart.

What Did You Learn?

- A planet is a body that revolves around the sun in a certain orbit.
- The planets would tend to move in a straight line away from the sun if the sun's gravitation did not pull the planets toward it.
- A system is any group whose members act on each other.
- The time it takes the earth to make one revolution around the sun is called a year.
- All planets rotate as they revolve around the sun.
- Day and night are caused by a planet's rotation.
- The seasons of a planet are caused by the planet's tilt as it revolves around the sun.
- Planets are not seen in the same place every night because they revolve around the sun at different speeds.

Biography

Nicolaus Copernicus (1473–1543)

Hundreds of years ago people pictured the earth at the center of their universe. They believed that the sun, moon, stars, and planets revolved around the earth.

However, in the 1500's the Polish astronomer **Copernicus** [kuh-Pur-nuh-kuhs] offered a new picture of how the universe is arranged. He believed that the sun, not the earth, was the center around which all planets revolved. Copernicus carefully recorded, for many years, the changes he saw in the sky. On the basis of these records, he believed that the earth moved rapidly through space. Copernicus said that we don't feel the earth moving because we are moving along with it. The moving earth causes the changes we see in the sky.

This was such a new idea that Copernicus waited until 1543 to print his work. It took many years of bitter fighting before people accepted this idea.

Now people think of the earth as just one member of a system of planets revolving around the sun. We think of Copernicus as the founder of present-day astronomy.

TO THINK ABOUT AND DO

Try to put these letters together in a way so that they form three words that are names of objects in the solar system.

WHAT DO YOU REMEMBER?

Copy these sentences on a piece of paper. Write **T** for each sentence that is true and **F** for each sentence that is false.

1. A planet's path is called its orbit.
2. The sun's gravitation pulls the planets toward it.
3. All planets rotate as they revolve around the sun.
4. The seasons are caused by a planet's rotation.
5. Planets appear to wander among the stars because they revolve around the sun at different speeds.
6. A planet's day is the time it takes for it to rotate one time.
7. The sun, the planets, and the asteroids form a system called the solar system.

Make up a puzzle like this one and try it on your friends. The answer should be a science word in this chapter.

> It is really a star, but we do not think of it as one. It is very large and hot. It gives heat and light to the earth. What is it?

ACTIVITY

You can make a model that will give you an idea of how large the sun is compared to the earth. You will need a large piece of cardboard, a meterstick, scissors, and some paste.

Cut out a circle that is 66.5 cm in diameter. This circle will be a model of the sun. Then cut out a circle that is 0.6 cm across. This circle will stand for the earth. Paste this small circle in the middle of the larger one.

Now draw a line through the middle of the sun circle. Paste as many cut-out earths as you can along this line. How many earth models were needed to equal the width of one sun model?

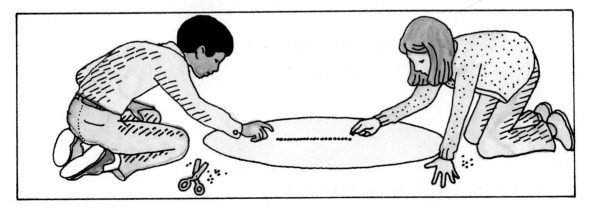

Traveling Through the Solar System

7

How exciting it must have been for this man to walk on the moon! He is one of few that have been able to gather information firsthand about its surface.

Have you ever wondered what it would be like on another planet? Soon you may know. Scientists are finding out new things about the solar system almost every day. They study the planets through powerful **telescopes** [TEHL-uh-skohps]. They receive information by radio from unmanned spacecraft traveling through the solar system. They also receive pictures taken by cameras on the spacecraft.

Imagine that scientists have found a way to send you safely through the solar system. How would you like to be among the first to visit one of the planets? There are only a few seats left on board the spacecraft. Would you like to come along?

photo at left: An astronaut explores the moon's surface.

Traveling to the Planets
Closest to the Sun

Our roaring rocket engines have just lifted us off the ground. Let's look back at the earth as we leave it. As we rise above the clouds in the earth's atmosphere, we see the patchwork pattern of the land areas on the earth's surface.

Now we can see brown areas that cover about one-fourth of the planet. In some places these areas are smooth. In others they are rough and marked by steep mountains. We can see many green patches among the brown areas. This is a sign that plant life is found on the earth. Blue areas cover the other parts of the planet. Can you think what these areas might be? From our spacecraft, what does Earth look like to you?

above: Saturn rocket lifting off from Cape Canaveral
left: Astronaut's view of Earth. Can you see Africa and the Arabian peninsula?

208

From this faraway view, what makes you think that you are looking at two planets? What we are really looking at is the earth and its **moon,** about one-fourth the size of the earth. It is not the only moon we shall see on our journey through the solar system. Moons move around some of the other planets. They move in much the same way that planets move around the sun.

The earth's moon has no atmosphere. It does have flat places, mountains, and bowl-shaped holes called **craters** [KRAY-tuhrz]. Scientists think that the craters were formed when objects from space crashed into the moon.

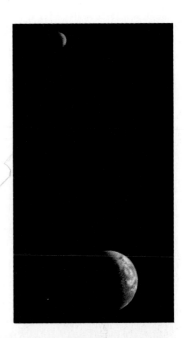

Surface of the moon

We are traveling through the solar system with great speed. After only 128 days of flight, we see the planet that is closest to the sun. It is covered with craters like the ones we saw on the moon. The planet is Mercury.

The planet Mercury. Notice the craters on the lighted side.

Artist's view of the surface of Mercury

Mercury is very dry and hot and has almost no atmosphere. The sun, now only about 58,000,000 km away, appears more than twice as large as it did on Earth. And the sun's heat and light energy is several times stronger here! Mercury doesn't have enough atmosphere to block out heat energy from the sun. The rocks and metals that we find here look as if they have been scorched.

Suppose we could land on the day side of Mercury. Our instruments measure the planet's temperature at about 500° C. We would wait about 88 Earth days before we could measure Mercury's temperature at night. That is the length of time it takes Mercury to rotate! Instead, we will fly by the night side of Mercury and measure its temperature on the way to the next planet. From what you have seen, do you think that life as we know it on Earth could be found on Mercury?

Since you left Mercury, you have been in flight for about 70 Earth days. You are looking at the planet Venus from a distance of about 5,000 km. From here, Venus is more than three times brighter than Earth would be from this distance. For many years, people believed that Venus was the earth's twin, since the two planets are very close in size.

Venus with its thick cloud cover

Venus shines brightly with a yellowish color. However, all we can see of the planet is a thick cloud cover. Much of the sun's energy seems to go through these clouds. This energy is trapped inside by a thick atmosphere of carbon dioxide.

The surface temperature of Venus may reach 480° C. This is much hotter than the highest temperature setting on a kitchen oven! Can you think why Earth's plants and animals could not live on Venus?

Our instruments show that the surface of Venus is somewhat like the surface of the earth. There are high mountains and many flat areas. One major discovery is a huge canyon that cuts across the planet. It is many times larger than the Grand Canyon on Earth. There is also a huge **volcano** [vahl-KAY-noh] on Venus. If future flights find that this 700-km opening is indeed a volcano, it could be bigger than any other volcano in the solar system.

Venus is the only planet that rotates opposite to the direction in which it travels around the sun. We will not be able to watch this rotation, however. This is because Venus rotates so slowly.

A drawing of the surface of Venus based on information gathered by United States and Soviet spacecraft

The Red Planet

From Venus, it will take about 170 Earth days to travel to Mars. After about 58 days, we see the blue water, brown land, and white clouds of Earth once more. Because of the earth's distance from the sun, it is neither totally hot and dry nor totally cold and frozen. At 155,000,000 km from the sun, the earth is probably the only planet that has life as we know it.

The planet Earth with its clouds, oceans, and land masses

Soon we begin to see yellow-orange in Mars' bright areas and gray-red in its dark areas. The bright areas are dry, desertlike places and are covered with dust. These are the areas that give Mars its red color when you look at the planet from the earth. The dark, higher areas are called "seas," even though they are not filled with water.

The red planet Mars

As you get closer to Mars, you will see channels that look like dry river beds, sand dunes, low hills, and craters. You will also see volcanoes and ice caps, which cover small areas at the planet's north and south poles. These ice caps are mostly water-ice with some frozen carbon dioxide. The red glow in the sky is caused by fine red dust trapped in the atmosphere. Sometimes great winds blow and make huge dust storms. These storms may last for several weeks.

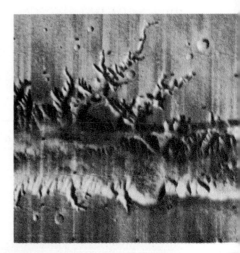

Surface of Mars

Mars photographed from space

The tilt of Mars causes the sun to heat the planet's northern and southern halves unequally. This is why Mars has seasons and the planet's temperature changes. The seasons on Mars last twice as long as they do on the earth. This is because Mars takes almost twice as long to go around the sun as the earth does. Since Mars is farther from the sun than the earth, temperatures here are generally lower than temperatures on Earth. In fact, the average temperature of the planet is $-70\,°C$!

If you could stay on Mars, you would see parts of the dark areas become lighter in color or disappear as the seasons changed. Scientists once believed that some form of plant life caused the changes in the dark areas. They believed that as the plants grew and then died, the color and size of the dark areas changed. Today, most scientists think the changes are caused by blowing sand and dust that cover and uncover parts of the surface. With the changing seasons, you would also see each polar cap get bigger and then smaller.

As we leave Mars, we look back at two small, strangely shaped moons which orbit the planet. Each looks like a football that has no air inside it.

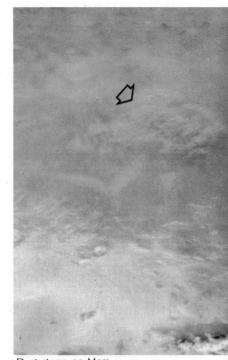

Dust storm on Mars

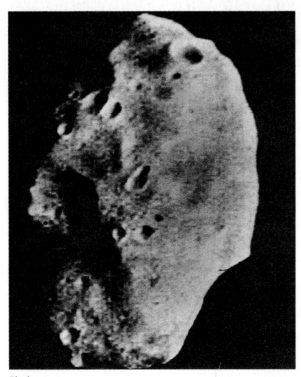

Phobos

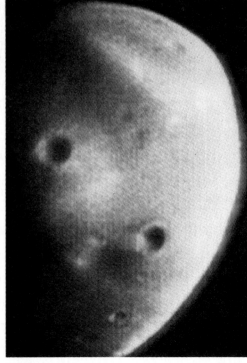

Deimos

217

Beyond Mars to a Giant

Some 180 days from Mars, we come upon a big chunk of rock and metal floating in space. At 5 km across, it is almost as big as one of the moons of Mars! After looking at our maps, we learn that we are moving through a part of the solar system known as the **asteroid belt** [AS-tuh-royd behlt]. In this belt, there are thousands of asteroids, each with a different shape and size. Most asteroids are no more than 1.6 km across. And countless numbers range down to the size of dust grains. Each asteroid is made of rock and metal and revolves around the sun between the orbits of Mars and Jupiter.

Geographos Asteroid

The asteroids orbit between Mars and Jupiter.

It will take us about 250 days to cross the asteroid belt. Will it be a dangerous trip? Will one of the asteroids hit our spacecraft? This is not likely. The asteroids are very far apart. Our spacecraft will probably not come near another one during the rest of our trip through the belt.

No one really knows how the asteroids were formed. They may be pieces of rock and metal that never became a planet. Most asteroids stay in the asteroid belt and orbit the sun. Sometimes, however, they enter the earth's atmosphere and burn up. As they burn, they leave a glowing trail of gas and dust as they fall toward Earth.

Meteor entering the earth's atmosphere

Two Earth years have passed since we left Mars. Far from the asteroid belt, our spacecraft nears the planet Jupiter. Earth is now a tiny dot against the blackness of space, and the sun is but a small yellow circle.

The planet Jupiter and two of its moons

When we look at Jupiter, we can see why it is called the giant planet. It is more than 11 times wider than Earth! Jupiter's mass is two and one-half times greater than the mass of all the other planets put together. With at least 16 moons revolving around it, Jupiter is like the center of a smaller solar system. And there may be other things around the huge planet, as well! A bright line in one of our pictures shows a thin, flat ring of matter that circles the planet.

Jupiter's ring

220

As we go by, our cameras take pictures of Jupiter's rapidly changing atmosphere. From these pictures, we can tell that Jupiter's atmosphere is made of moving bands of colored clouds. Yellows, whites, oranges, blues, and browns wrap the planet like giant ribbons. These strangely moving bands get wider and then more narrow as they combine and break up. See the twisted whirls of color between the rushing bands of clouds! Storms larger than our entire planet also whirl across the surface of Jupiter.

A close-up of Jupiter's atmosphere

Jupiter's Red Spot—a huge storm

No one knows how Jupiter's Great Red Spot came to be. Many scientists think the Red Spot, which is really orange in color, is a huge storm like a **hurricane** [HUR-uh-kayn]. Can you imagine a "spot" that is larger than several Earths?

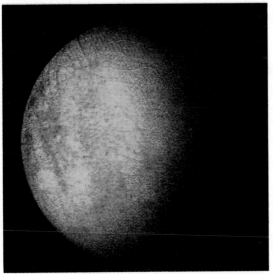

Europa   Ganymede

We have far more to see than the planet Jupiter itself. We shall try to learn more about Jupiter's four large moons, two of which have ice on their surfaces. The moons with icy surfaces are like watery Earths that have been frozen. The frozen crust of one of these moons has many lines running across its surface. These lines may be cracks caused when the layers below the surface moved and pushed upward. While we look at another moon, notice the hot matter flowing out of its volcanoes. Outside of the earth, this is the first time that active volcanoes have been found in our solar system.

During the flyby, we use Jupiter's huge gravitation to speed us up and direct us toward the next planet—Saturn. Since we will be in flight for five Earth years before reaching Saturn, we will have much time to gather information about space.

Calisto

Io

More Ringed Planets

We are nearing one of the most beautiful sights in the solar system. Sunlight shining on the planet Saturn makes it glow with a dull yellowish color. And the gleaming white of its rings looks like many shining diamonds. When early scientists looked at Saturn through their telescopes, they thought the planet had an "ear" on each side. When more powerful telescopes were made, scientists saw that the "ears" were simply the shining rings.

The planet Saturn and its rings

A close-up of Saturn's rings

The rings that circle Saturn are found about 11,000 km above the planet and extend into space for more than 64,000 km. The rings are made of water-ice or ice-covered bits of rock. Each piece is like a tiny moon orbiting Saturn. No one knows where the rings of Saturn came from. They may be pieces of matter that once tried to form a moon. If the moon got too close to Saturn's strong gravitation, it may have been torn to pieces.

Most scientists believe that Saturn has no real surface. Because of its thick cloud cover, it is hard to tell exactly where the atmosphere ends and Saturn begins. The gases that form Saturn's atmosphere are probably found inside the planet as well. The pressure is so great inside Saturn, however, that the gases may be in a solid form.

Saturn takes about 29 times longer than Earth to make one revolution around the sun. Saturn rotates faster than any other planet except Jupiter, however. It makes one turn about every ten hours. What a short day!

Saturn and several of its moons

Besides its rings, Saturn has more than 20 moons revolving around it. The largest of these moons is between the size of Mercury and Mars. Can you imagine being on Saturn and seeing all these moons in the sky? This is, of course, if you could see through Saturn's thick atmosphere.

It will take us another five and a half years to reach Uranus, the seventh planet in the solar system. The pale green planet Uranus has five moons that revolve around it. Do you see the rings that also circle the planet?

Compare the tilt of Uranus with the tilt of Earth.

Scientists know little about the surface of Uranus. It looks as if there are clouds all around the planet. Since Uranus receives so little of the sun's energy, the planet must be very cold and covered with frozen gases.

Unlike the other planets, Uranus lies on its side in its orbit around the sun. One orbit—a Uranus year—is 84 Earth years long. If you could look into space from one of the poles of Uranus, you would see the sun for 42 Earth years. You would then live in darkness for another 42 years.

On to the Planets Farthest from the Sun

As we travel toward the next planet, we see a faint, starlike object headed toward the sun. This object may be made of rock, gases, and ice mixed together so that it looks like a dirty snowball! We are looking at a **comet** [KAHM-iht].

As it moves nearer the sun, the comet becomes brighter and brighter. When the comet comes within Jupiter's orbit, the sun's energy forces its body to get bigger and its gases to evaporate. The gases, along with some solid pieces, often sweep out in a kind of tail. The tail is always pushed away from the sun. Energy from the sun causes the material in the comet's head and tail to give off light.

An artist's view of the planet Neptune

Ahead of us we see the planet Neptune. Neptune looks like a blue-green ball against the blackness of space. All we can see is its thick, cloudy atmosphere. Our instruments tell us that the average temperature of the planet is about −170 °C.

Neptune was **predicted** [prih-DIHKT-ehd] before it was ever seen! Scientists had noticed that Uranus was not orbiting the sun the way they thought it should. The gravitational pull of some unknown planet seemed to be the cause of Uranus' strange movements. In 1864 Neptune, along with its two moons, was seen for the first time through a telescope.

An artist's view of the planet Pluto

Most of the time, Pluto has been at the edge of the solar system. But in 1979, Pluto's orbit moved inside that of Neptune. Pluto will remain the eighth planet from the sun until 1999. Then it will once again move outside Neptune's orbit.

It would take more than 20 earth years for you to travel to Pluto. Pluto is about one fourth as large as Earth. Since it receives little energy from the sun, it is very cold and icy. Scientists believe that Pluto has one moon.

Pluto, like Neptune, was predicted before it was seen. One scientist pointed a telescope toward the place where he thought the unknown planet would be. He placed a camera on the part of the telescope that he looked through. In 1930 he was able to find Pluto by comparing pictures taken 24 hours apart.

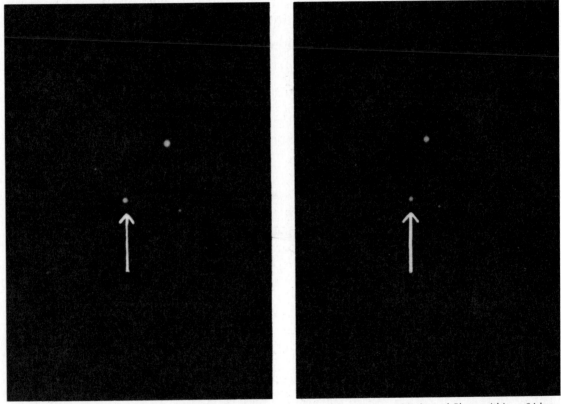

Motion of Pluto within a 24-hour period

Think about all the planets that you saw on this trip. Each planet moved in its own orbit and at its own speed. What if you were able to travel far beyond our solar system? What do you think the solar system would look like from outer space?

You can find out what our solar system looks like by making a model of it. You will need a metric ruler, a piece of paper, and a crayon. You and your classmates together will also need one large sheet of paper, a long string, and a meter-stick.

How big should you make the planets in your model? Is the planet Earth bigger than Venus? Or is it the same size? It's not easy to tell about sizes by looking at a picture. Use your ruler and crayon to make a straight line that is 1 cm long on your paper. Draw a circle around this line. You have made a model planet—the planet Earth!

	Diameter Scale			Diameter Scale
Sun	109 cm		Jupiter	11.1 cm
Mercury	0.4 cm		Saturn	9.4 cm
Venus	0.9 cm		Uranus	4.0 cm
Earth	1.0 cm		Neptune	3.9 cm
Mars	0.5 cm		Pluto	0.5 cm

This chart shows how wide each of the other model planets should be compared to the earth. Pick any planet and make a model of it. When you have finished, put your planet next to the other planets. Can you tell which planet is the biggest? Which is the smallest? Which planets are about the same size?

You and your friends have made models of all the planets in the solar system. But something is missing! Do you know what part of the solar system you have left out?

Now get together with your classmates. On the large sheet of paper, make a circle that is 109 cm wide. Use the long string and a crayon to help you draw the outline. You have made a model sun. Compare this model to the model planets. Do you see how much bigger the sun really is?

Are the planets and the sun close together as they move in space? Not at all! Each planet is moving in its own orbit at a different distance from the sun. If you are going to make a model of the solar system, you must be sure that no two planets are the same distance from the sun. How can you do this?

This chart shows how far from the sun each planet should be. Keep in mind that the distances in your model are billions of times smaller than the distances in space.

	Distance km	Scale Distance m
Sun	0	0
Mercury	58,000,000	0.4
Venus	108,000,000	0.7
Earth	150,000,000	1.0
Mars	228,000,000	1.5
Jupiter	778,000,000	5.2
Saturn	1,427,000,000	9.6
Uranus	2,869,000,000	19.4
Neptune	4,497,000,000	30.1
Pluto	5,900,000,000	39.8

Take this chart, a meterstick, your model sun, and the planets, and go outside. Have someone hold the model sun at one end of a long sidewalk. Use your meterstick and the chart to measure how far from the sun your planet is. Then stand at this spot holding your model planet for everyone to see.

Make believe you are really standing on this planet. What does the earth look like from where you are? Look at the planets that other students are holding. What do they look like from where you are? Is the sun hard to see from where you are standing? Change places with someone who has another planet and make believe you are on that planet now. How have things changed?

In 1903, the Wright brothers flew the first powered, heavier-than-air craft. It flew 37 meters and stayed in the air for 12 seconds. In 1981, John Young and Robert Crippen flew the first test flight of the space shuttle. Think of the changes that have taken place in air travel in just 78 years.

The space shuttle orbiter is 37 meters long and has a wingspan of about 24 meters. At lift-off, the space shuttle weighs 1,995,840 kg. The Wright brothers' plane weighed only 340 kg.

The shuttle looks more like a jet airplane than a rocket. At lift-off, each shuttle includes a large fuel tank and two solid rocket boosters, which power the craft into orbit. Since the shuttle can be used over and over again, it can make many return trips into outer space.

Flight deck of a space shuttle

The first 40 flights of the space shuttle have already been booked. Many flights will have people from different countries, colleges, and companies working together.

Shuttles will be used to bring people and things into outer space. While in outer space, other smaller spacecraft will be lifted from the shuttle's holds and placed in orbit. Scientific experiments will be carried out. Even space stations can be built from things brought into space by the shuttle.

Would you like to be part of the space shuttle crew and travel into outer space?

What Did You Learn?

- Mercury, the planet nearest the sun, is dry and hot, and has many surface craters.
- Venus is a hot, cloud-covered planet whose surface has mountains, flat places, canyons, and volcanoes.
- Earth is the only planet whose changes in temperature, distance from the sun, and amount of liquid water make life as we know it possible.
- Mars is a dry, desertlike planet whose surface has channels, dunes, hills, and craters. As the seasons on Mars change, there are differences in the dark areas and in the polar ice caps.
- Asteroids are planetlike objects of rock and metal in orbit between Mars and Jupiter.
- Jupiter, the largest planet, has the Great Red Spot in its whirling clouds and holds at least 16 moons in orbit.
- Saturn has more than 20 moons and several rings of water-ice or ice-covered bits of rock that revolve around it.
- Uranus, the pale green planet with five moons, lies on its side as it orbits the sun.
- A comet becomes brighter as it travels toward the sun.
- Neptune and Pluto, the planets farthest from the sun, were predicted before they were seen.
- The space shuttle can be used for many return trips to outer space.

Biography

Dr. Ronald E. McNair (1950–   )

The idea of people living and working in space is no longer something from science fiction. The space shuttle will be carrying more trained people and equipment to study Earth than ever before. Scientists will be able to answer questions that astronomers have been asking for a long time. They will be better able to understand how our universe works. One such scientist is Dr. Robert E. McNair.

"Being an astronaut is something that I've always thought about," said Dr. McNair. He was one of the first 35 people chosen by the National Aeronautics and Space Administration (NASA) for shuttle flights. He is a scientist who studied physics. He trained for two years at the Johnson Space Center, beginning with classroom work. This training was followed by learning all of the details of the shuttle's system.

As a mission specialist, Mr. McNair might take space walks, do experiments, or help keep the spacecraft in working order.

TO THINK ABOUT AND DO

WORD FUN

On a piece of paper copy the letters below the pictures of objects found in the solar system. From the list below, choose the name of the correct object and write it next to each letter.

Sun	Mars	Pluto	Jupiter	Neptune	Saturn
Earth	Comet	Venus	Asteroids	Uranus	Mercury

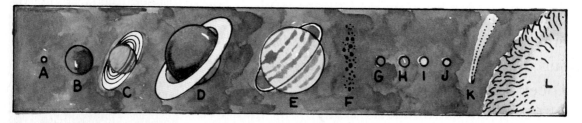

WHAT DO YOU REMEMBER?

On a piece of paper copy the sentences. Choose the planet from the list that best fits each description and write its number after the sentence.

1. Which planet is the largest—1, 7, or 4?
2. We now know that several planets have rings. Of the following planets, which one has rings—6, 9, or 3?
3. Which planet appears to be reddish because of its bright, desertlike places—4, 2, or 1?
4. Which is the only planet that supports life as we know it—8, 1, or 9?
5. Which planet has the highest temperature—9, 4, or 8?

1. Mars
2. Neptune
3. Pluto
4. Mercury
5. Uranus
6. Saturn
7. Jupiter
8. Venus
9. Earth

Some of the planets were named for Greek and Roman gods. Which ones are they? What are some of the stories that tell how the planets got these names? You may need to use books from your classroom or library to find answers to these questions.

ACTIVITY

Suppose you are a space traveler studying the surface of the moon. You are out driving your moon rover, stopping to collect soil and rocks. Suddenly, while driving through a large crater, the moon rover becomes stuck. You must now walk back to the moon base, which is about 100 km away.

Before you make the long walk, you must decide on what things to take with you. Below is a list of things which you are able to find in the moon rover.

tubes of food	flashlight
40 m of rope	first-aid kit
oxygen tanks	star chart
2 liters of water	solar-powered radio

You will not be able to carry all of these things, and so you decide to take only four. List the four you would choose. Arrange the four from most important to least important. Then compare your list with the lists of other students.

Structures of Our Planet's Resources

Unit V

The Earth's Rocks

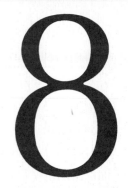

Have you ever wondered where a rock was formed? Was it once on the bottom of a sea? Or perhaps it was formed below the earth's surface. In some places inside the earth, great heat and pressure build up. In these places, the hot liquid below the surface may be forced out. The rock may have been part of this liquid rock that flowed out, cooled, and changed to a solid form. Or maybe the rock was part of a mountain. Sometimes pieces of a mountain are broken off and carried to other places by water, ice, or wind.

Have you ever found an interesting or unusual rock? Did it have specks of different colors on its surface? Was it smooth, or did it have rough edges? Maybe your rock had pieces of shells in it. Or perhaps you found a rock with parts of things that used to be alive inside it.

photo at left: El Capitan, a huge mass of granite found in Yosemite National Park, California

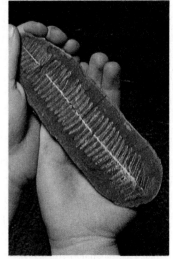

Fossil of leaf from fern plant

"Fire Rocks"

Do you know how hot pudding looks when it is poured into small dishes? In a short time, the top of the pudding cools and becomes solid. What happens when someone breaks through the surface of the pudding with a spoon? Do you think it will still be hot on the inside? Even though the top layer of the pudding has cooled, the part under it could burn your tongue!

How is pudding like the crust and magma?

The earth's crust is somewhat like the crust of the pudding. It too has had time to cool and has become solid. Under this thin layer, however, the temperature is very high. In fact, the temperature is so high under the earth's crust that the matter there is hot. In some places the matter is melted. We find that it is a thick liquid rock called **magma** [MAG-muh].

246

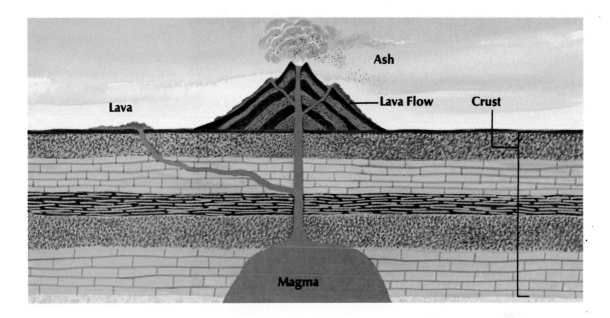

Inside the earth, the pressure is sometimes so high that the hot magma is forced through cracks in the earth's crust. When this happens, we have a volcano! A volcano is an opening in the earth's crust that allows liquid rock and gases to escape. The deposits of ash and rock that build up around the opening are part of the volcano as well. The hot, liquid rock that escapes from the opening may flood the land for kilometers around.

Once at the surface, the hot rock is called **lava** [LAV-uh]. Lava cools quickly and becomes solid rock. Some volcanic mountains form from the lava that builds up over the years. Others form quickly and suddenly. When magma, almost as thick as tar, bursts through the earth's surface, there are large amounts of volcanic dust and great noise.

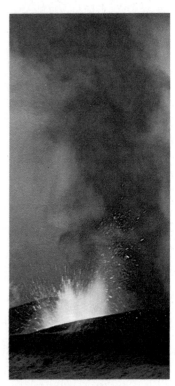

Surtsey erupting in Iceland

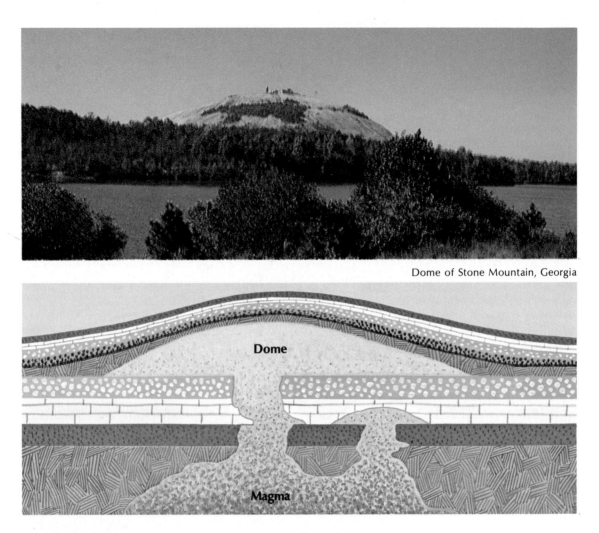

Dome of Stone Mountain, Georgia

Often, however, magma stays under the surface in huge pockets or in cracks in the crust. Here the liquid rock cools slowly. In fact, it takes thousands or even millions of years for this magma to become solid rock.

All rocks that were formed from fiery-hot magma, whether they cooled above or below the earth's surface, are called **igneous** [IHG-nee-uhs] rocks. Igneous means "fire-formed." Why, do you think, is this a good name for these rocks?

There are many kinds of igneous rocks. Each of these rocks is made of one or more **minerals** [MIHN-uhr-uhlz] that have combined in different ways and in different amounts. Some of the minerals look like colored glass. Others look dull and feel oily. Some minerals are hard enough to scratch glass. Others are so soft that you could scratch them with your own fingernail!

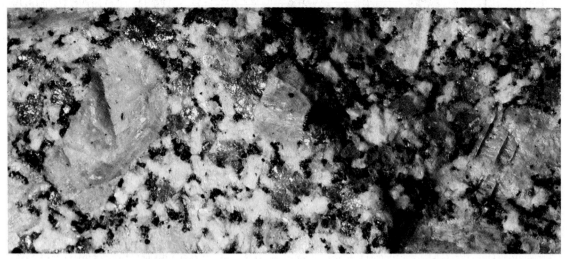

Granite

Let's look at some minerals that make up one kind of igneous rock. This rock is called **granite** [GRAN-iht]. Do you see the different-colored specks in this piece of granite? Each of these specks is a mineral. How many different minerals do you see in the granite?

How do you think the different minerals get into rocks like granite? To find the answer, we must return to magma. Magma is really a mixture of minerals in their liquid form. As magma cools, each of the different minerals is changed to its solid form. When this happens, the atoms of each mineral may take on a certain pattern that repeats itself many times.

Salt crystals

When this pattern has been repeated enough times so that it can be seen, we have a mineral **crystal** [KRIHS-tl].

Each crystal has a certain number of smooth, flat sides. What shape is each side of these salt crystals? How many sides do they have?

How can a mineral in its liquid form be changed into a solid crystal? To find out, you will need a glass slide, an eyedropper, a liquid your teacher will give you, and a hand lens. You should also wear safety glasses.

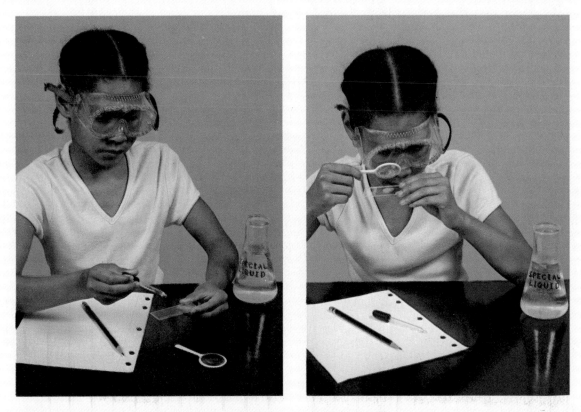

On your slide, put a few drops of the liquid that contains a certain mineral. Through your hand lens watch what happens to this liquid. Draw a sketch of the liquid after it cools. What is the shape of each crystal? How is each crystal like the ones you saw in granite? How is it different?

Rocks from Magma

Many kinds of igneous rocks can be formed from magma because magma is a mixture of many, many kinds of matter. The mixture of matter in magma is not the same throughout. In fact, the matter in the earth's magma can be mixed in an almost endless number of ways.

Here are three different kinds of igneous rocks. Even though each rock was formed from magma, you can see that none of the three looks alike. The reason is that not all of the same kinds of matter are present in each rock. Also, the amount of matter in each kind of rock is different.

You already know one of the rocks on page 252. Can you find it? It is granite. You were probably able to find it easily because you had already seen the different crystals that make up granite. When granite was formed, it did not come to the earth's surface. Instead, it cooled slowly under the surface. In this way, there was time for larger crystals to form.

When lava pours out of a volcano, it may cool very quickly on the surface of the earth. It may cool so quickly, in fact, that there is little time for crystals to form, and the rock is as smooth as glass. This quickly cooling rock is called **obsidian** [awb-SIHD-ee-uhn].

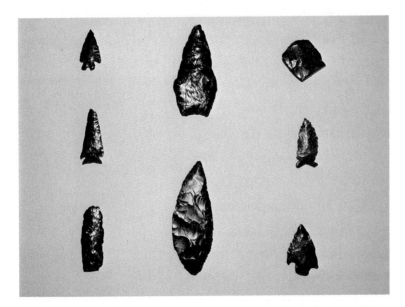

These arrowheads made of obsidian were once used as hunting weapons and tools.

Basalt [buh-SAWLT] is a hard, dark-colored igneous rock. Slower cooling of the lava on the earth's surface allowed time for tiny mineral crystals to "grow" inside it.

How does the time it takes magma to cool make a difference in the size of the crystal that forms? You will need three margarine tubs with covers, a shoe box of sand, three sheets of black paper, and a white crayon. You will also need two pans, one filled with ice water and the other filled with hot water, and safety glasses. Your teacher will give you a special liquid that contains minerals.

In the sand, make a hole that is large enough to hold one of the margarine tubs. Then ask your teacher to pour some of the special liquid into each of the tubs. Quickly place a cover on each tub.

Set one tub in the hot water and another in the ice water. Place the third tub in the hole that you made in the sand. Wait until the pan of hot water has cooled. Then remove each tub from the water or sand and take its top off. What do you notice inside each tub?

One at a time, remove the crystals from the tubs. Place them on a sheet of black paper and label the paper with your crayon. Then look at each group of crystals with your hand lens. How is each group different? What do you think made the difference?

left: Coarse-grained granite; *right:*
Fine-grained granite

When magma cools deep inside the earth, it
cools slowly and forms large crystals. When
magma cools more quickly, as it does in a lava
flow, the crystals are smaller.

Rocks from Broken Rocks

Is there a place in your neighborhood where there are many rocks on the ground? The rocks may look hard, but year after year, rain, ice, frost, and wind wear away their surfaces. Pieces of rock that are worn off may be washed into a stream that flows into a river. Bits of dead plants and animals may also be carried down into the water. Year after year, rivers carry these **sediments** [SEHD-uh-muhnts] from high places down to the sea.

left and center: Rivers carrying sediments
right: River depositing sediment in ocean

Sediments are deposited in layers. As millions of years go by, the lower layers become squeezed together by the many layers of matter above them. The pressure of all these layers is very great. The layers are pressed together so very hard that the lower layers stick together. Also, minerals in water moving through the layers may act much as a glue around the bits and pieces of sediment. Over millions of years these layers of sediment become solid rock.

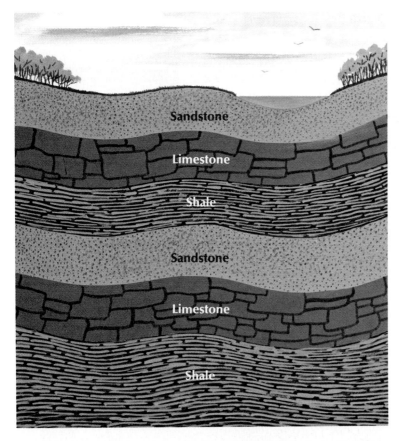

Sandstone

Limestone

Shale

Sandstone

Limestone

Shale

Sandstone

Limestone

Shale

Sand is only one of the many materials that settle to the bottom of the sea. Grains of clay, colorful rocks, bits of plants, skeletons of sea animals, and shells all settle in layers. Rock that is formed from this sediment is called **sedimentary** [sehd-uh-MEHN-tuhr-ee] rock.

Just as there are many different kinds of matter that make up the sediment, so there are different kinds of sedimentary rock. Most sedimentary rocks have been formed from layers of sediment that were squeezed together under great pressure. But these rocks are sometimes formed in other ways as well.

One group of sedimentary rock is formed from solid matter. This matter is broken up by water into pieces too tiny to be seen. When the water evaporates, the solid matter is left behind. Huge areas of rock salt were formed in this way. When the earth's surface changed, parts of the ocean evaporated. As this happened, layers of salt crystals were left behind.

Salt deposits in Death Valley, California

Another group of sedimentary rock is formed from the bodies of plants and animals that were once living. Coal is such a sedimentary rock. It is made up of plant matter that came under great pressure. Skeletons of sea animals millions of years old are sometimes found in **limestone** [LYM-stohn], another sedimentary rock.

Limestone with fossils

You can make one kind of sedimentary rock. You will need some sand, chalk, some water, and a paper cup. You will also need a piece of window screen, a piece of cloth, a hammer, and safety glasses.

Pour the sand through the window screen and collect the grains that fall through. Now wrap the chalk in the cloth and crush it with the hammer.

Place 1 spoonful of chalk and 5 spoonfuls of sand into the cup and mix them thoroughly. Now slowly add water to the mixture and stir until it becomes a paste. Then pack the mixture tightly into the bottom of the cup.

Let the mixture dry for at least 24 hours. After it is dry, tear away the paper cup. You have made a kind of sedimentary rock. Can you name what kind of rock it is?

Why is it that you can easily find sedimentary rocks, once at the bottom of the sea, on the ground in your neighborhood? Over the years, the land is worn away by wind, water, and ice. At the same time, sediments are building on the bottom of the sea. As the mass of the sediments becomes greater, more and more pressure is put on the rocks under the earth's surface. Forces within the earth cause the land to slowly rise. In this way, the land is lifted to greater heights.

How sediments cause a change in the land.

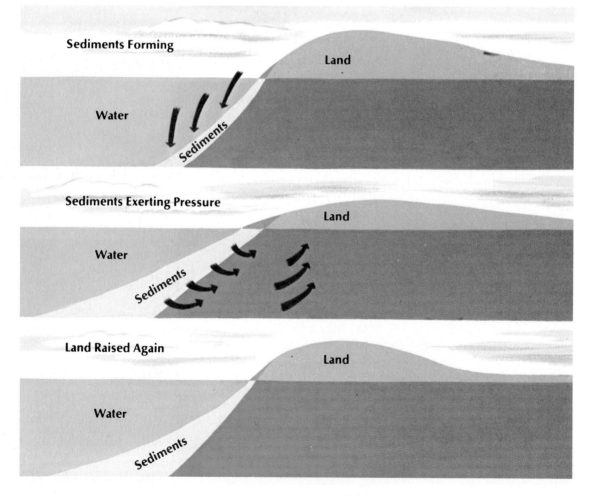

Sediments Forming

Land

Water

Sediments

Sediments Exerting Pressure

Land

Water

Sediments

Land Raised Again

Land

Water

Sediments

Clues to the Past from Sedimentary Rocks

Every rock gives us clues to the past. Sedimentary rocks give us some very important clues. Sediments are deposited in layers. The layers may cover dead plants and animals, protecting them for millions of years. As the sediments are changed to rock, either the remains or the outlines of the plants and animals can still be seen. The "clues" of past plant and animal life that can be seen in the rock are known as **fossils** [FAHS-uhlz].

Fossil remains may be bones, teeth, or the hard coverings of plants and animals. Fossil prints may be footprints of animals or the outlines of leaves, insects, or shells. Fossils help us understand something of the past. Some fossils, like those of the **dinosaur** [DY-nuh-sawr] and the saber-toothed tiger, help us tell a story about strange animals that no longer live on the earth. Fossil water plants found on a mountain top also give clues to the earth's changes.

Seashell fossils

Dinosaur bones found on mountaintop in Colorado

Dinosaur track near Moab, Utah

Here is a way to make a model of a fossil. You will need some clay, some cooking oil, a paper cup, and a spoon. Also get some plaster, some water, a shell or a bone, and a piece of foil.

Lay the clay on the foil. Flatten the clay with your hands. Lightly coat the shell or the bone with oil. Press the object into the clay with enough force to make a mold. Then carefully remove the object from the clay. Mix some plaster with the water. Pour this mixture into the mold that you made. Then set the mold aside for two to three hours.

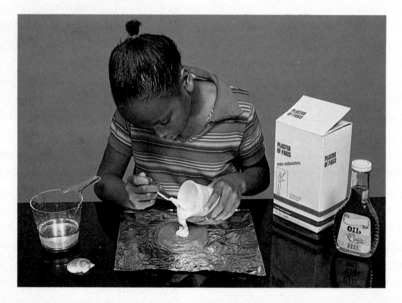

Carefully take the clay away from the hardened plaster. Which material, the clay or the plaster, stands for the shell or the bone itself? Which material is the fossil of the shell or the bone?

Fossils are most often found in limestone, although they may be found in other soft sedimentary rocks such as **shale** [shayl] and **sandstone** [SAND-stohn]. Why do you think seashells or their prints are found more often than fossils of land animals? The reason is that ocean sediments cover dead sea animals fairly quickly. On land, however, a plant or an animal is less likely to be covered by sediment. It is usually eaten first. Or it may become part of the soil.

Fern fossils in shale

Brachiopod fossils in sandstone

Fish fossils

Sometimes animals were caught in bogs or in tar pits like the **La Brea** [lah BRAY-uh] pits in Los Angeles. There, animals were caught in the hot tar. The tar cooled around the trapped animals and became solid.

Statues of prehistoric animals in La Brea tar pits

263

Scientists have also found complete remains of animals that were frozen when they fell into cracks in deep ice. This animal had died thousands of years ago. But parts of its flesh and skin were still on its skeleton!

A whole plant is hardly ever found as a fossil. In some places, however, tree trunks were buried under sand, mud, and volcanic ash. After millions of years, some groups of these trunks are still standing. Minerals from the sand, mud, and ash caused the trunks to **petrify** [PEHT-ruh-fy], or become solid rock.

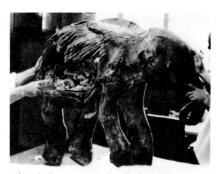

This baby mammoth died 10,000 years ago during the last Ice Age. Its body was found frozen in an excavation area in Siberia.

Petrified wood

Rocks That Are Changed

Both igneous and sedimentary rock can be changed into a different kind of rock. Over millions of years, pressure and heat cause changes in these rocks. Rocks that have been changed by heat and pressure are called **metamorphic** [meht-uh-MOHR-fihk] rocks.

You have seen changes caused by heat and pressure. In a few minutes you can change two pieces of bread and a slice of cheese into a toasted cheese sandwich. In a few million years, heat and pressure can change rock too. Then it will be different in color, in hardness, and in the smoothness of its surface.

left: Collection of shells on beach; *center:* Sedimentary layers in limestone; *right:* Sheets of marble

Marble is a smooth metamorphic rock that has many shiny crystals. It is formed from limestone, a sedimentary rock that is somewhat softer. Inside the earth, where the temperature is very high, bits of shell in the limestone are changed into the fine shiny crystals we see in marble.

left: Dried mud; *center:* Shale; *right:* Slate

Shale is a sedimentary rock made from layers of mud that have come under much pressure. When shale is heated and pressed beneath the earth's surface for many years, it may be changed to **slate** [slayt], a hard, smooth metamorphic rock.

Igneous rocks can also be changed. You know that granite was once melted rock, like lava, but did not cool on the earth's surface. It cooled slowly under the surface and formed fairly large crystals as it hardened. **Gneiss** [nys] is a metamorphic rock made of the same minerals as granite. However, it is formed when granite is heated under great pressure inside the earth. The minerals in granite melt together and cool, forming the bands of color that you see in gneiss.

left: Lava; *center:* Fine-grained granite; *right:* Granite gneiss

Erupting volcano in Hawaii

There are many other kinds of metamorphic rocks made by heat and pressure. What do you think makes the heat that melts and changes rocks?

Some rocks are heated by magma or other hot materials deep within the earth. Or they may be heated on the earth's surface when magma and water vapor escape from a volcano.

Building Up and Wearing Away

Ancient people believed that because rocks are so hard, they do not change. Now we know that this is not true. It just takes a long time! Minute by minute, year after year, the earth's rocks are being changed in ways that are hard to see.

Heat and pressure change igneous and sedimentary rock to metamorphic rock. Over and over, rocks build up and wear away. This building up and wearing away of rock is called the **rock cycle** [rahk SY-kuhl]. In this never-ending cycle, rocks are changed from one kind to another.

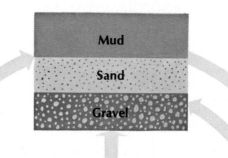

Mud

Sand

Gravel

Igneous Rock

Metamorphic Rock

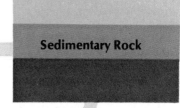

Sedimentary Rock

Magma

Magma, the rock-forming liquid, cools and hardens into igneous rock. Igneous rock is broken and scratched and ground into pebbles, sand, and even smaller rock pieces. All these materials may become sediments on the bottom of the sea. There, they may be squeezed and "glued" together and changed to sedimentary rock. Sometimes the sea bottom is pushed up. When this happens, the sedimentary rock becomes part of the land, which will be shaped by water, ice, or wind. As pieces of the sedimentary rock are worn away, they are moved by streams and rivers to the sea. There the cycle begins again.

The rock cycle takes millions of years. Air, water, heat, ice, and pressure all act to change the earth's rocks. What will today's sedimentary rock be changed into? After millions of years, will it be a metamorphic rock high in a mountain range? Or will it be melted to form magma flowing from a fiery volcano?

Grand Tetons, Wyoming

What Did You Learn?

- Igneous rocks are formed from magma.
- Rocks are made of one or more kinds of matter that have combined in different ways and in different amounts.
- The time it takes igneous rocks to cool makes a difference in the size of the crystals that form.
- Over many years, sedimentary rocks are formed when bits of rock and dead plants and animals are squeezed together by the pressure of layers of sediment above.
- When sediment is deposited over dead plants and animals, they are changed to rock after millions of years. In this way, fossils are formed.
- Metamorphic rocks are formed when rocks are changed by heat and pressure.
- The earth's rocks are always being built up and worn away in the rock cycle.

Career

Geologist

There is much to know about the materials that make up the earth and the forces that shape it. People who try to explain how the earth was formed and how it changes are called **geologists** [jee-AHL-uh-jihsts].

Geologists can look at a mountain and tell how it was made. They can tell whether it was pushed up by the force of an active volcano or made by the shaking of an earthquake. They can tell other ways that mountains are made. A geologist can look at a piece of rock, perhaps a million years old, and tell us about it. Geologists study soils, rivers, and other parts of the earth.

Many geologists travel all over the world. Some search for coal, oil, and gas on land or under the ocean. Others go into mines, looking for deposits that have metals and gems in them.

Many geologists teach or work for companies, for the government, or in museums.

TO THINK ABOUT AND DO

WORD FUN

On a piece of paper copy the names of the different kinds of rocks listed in Column A. For each rock on your list, choose the group to which it belongs from Column B and write the name of this group beside it.

Column A	Column B
granite	
sandstone	igneous
slate	
marble	sedimentary
limestone	
basalt	metamorphic

WHAT DO YOU REMEMBER?

In each sentence below, a science word is missing. Copy each sentence on a piece of paper. Then choose the correct word to finish it.

1. Igneous rocks are formed from _____.
2. Every rock is made of one or more _____.
3. The remains of plants or animals that have been preserved in rock are _____.
4. Rocks that are formed when igneous and sedimentary rocks are changed by heat and pressure are _____.
5. The earth's rocks are always being built up and worn away in the _____.
6. When a mineral's atoms take on a pattern that repeats itself enough times to be seen, we have a _____.

fossils
metamorphic
rock cycle
crystal
magma
minerals

272

Which group of rocks listed in the chart can become other groups of rocks? Copy the names of the rock materials in the chart. Next to each name, write the names of the kind of rock that each rock can change to.

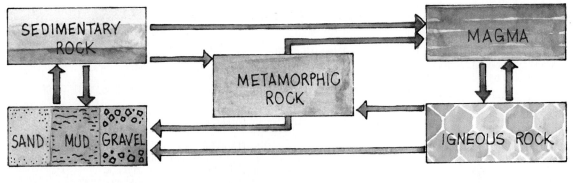

ACTIVITY

What will form on the string? To find out, you will need some water, some salt, a pan, a pencil, a nail, and 20 cm of string. You will also need a glass or other clear bowl, a spoon, a source of heat, a measuring cup and a magnifying lens.

Boil one cup of water in the pan. Pour in a half cup of salt. Stir until you can no longer see the salt. Then remove the pan from the heat.

Pour the warm salt water from the pan into a clean glass or bowl. Tie a nail to a string and then tie the string to a pencil. Place the nail in the glass, as you see here.

Allow the salt water to cool for about an hour. Then look at the string. What do you see? What is the shape of the crystals? Use a magnifying lens to help you see the separate crystals.

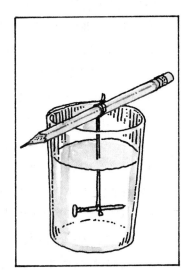

273

Sunlight and Green Plants

9

It feels so good to be in the warm sunlight. If only you didn't feel so hungry. If you could just stay there and eat the sunlight! But you can't do it no matter how hard you try. So you do the next best thing. You eat the sunlight in another form, in food. Every bite of your food was made with energy from sunlight. You can't see it, feel it, or taste it, but the energy of sunlight is there.

photo at left: Enjoying the sunshine

275

Food-Making in Green Plants

You could lie in the sunlight all day long, and you would just become hungrier and hungrier. But the green plants all around you can do something very wonderful with the same sunlight. They can use the energy of sunlight to make food. The leaves and the other green parts of the plant make the food that feeds the whole plant. When you eat green plants, your body gets the energy it needs.

Vegetable farm

Green seems to be an important color for plants. Why is it so important? Green is the color of the food-making material in plants. Green plants make their own food out of materials in the soil and in the air. This food is made by a green material called **chlorophyll** [KLOHR-uh-fihl].

Chlorophyll gives leaves their green color.

A green leaf is really a small food factory. Perhaps you have visited a big food factory, such as a bread bakery. You know that there is a stream of raw materials, such as flour, sugar, and salt, entering the factory. Machines mix the raw materials into dough. The heat energy from the oven bakes the dough into the finished product—bread. The finished product is carried to a place where it is kept until it is needed.

The same thing happens in a leaf, the little food factory of a plant. Two streams of raw materials enter from two directions. Water and minerals are the raw materials from the soil. The other raw material is carbon dioxide from the air. The energy to run the factory is sunlight. The minerals are needed to start the food-making. In the sunlight, the water and the carbon dioxide are worked on by the green chlorophyll. The main finished product is sugar. When this goes on, something else is produced—oxygen. The oxygen goes into the air and puts back the oxygen used by most living things.

Food-making in green plants is called **photosynthesis** [foh-toh-SIHN-thuh-sihs]. *Photo* means "light." *Synthesis* means "putting together." Photosynthesis does not take place at night or in dark caves. It does not take place deep in the sea where light from the sun cannot reach. Photosynthesis can take place only in light.

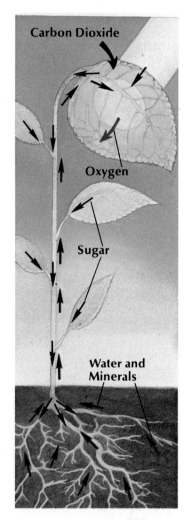

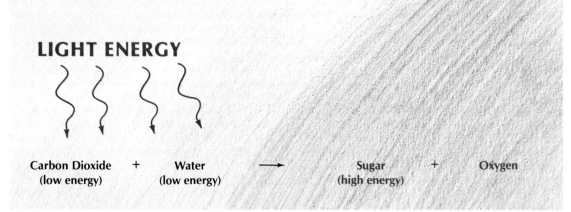

LIGHT ENERGY

Carbon Dioxide (low energy) + Water (low energy) → Sugar (high energy) + Oxygen

Photosynthesis

278

Water for Photosynthesis

Let's see how the raw materials needed for making sugar finally get to the leaf.

Have you ever tried to pull a large green plant from the ground? You know that it can be a lot of hard work. The roots hold the plant in place.

But roots do something more than hold the plant in place. You know that a plant needs water for photosynthesis. But how does the plant get this water? Let's look at some roots and see if you can find out.

A carrot is the root of a carrot plant. The carrot has many thin tubes through which water can move up to the stems and leaves. But the carrot also has an outside layer through which the water and minerals cannot easily soak. How does the water get into the carrot then? Let's look more closely. Do you see some thinner and smaller roots? Water and minerals can move into these thin roots.

Roots absorb water and minerals.

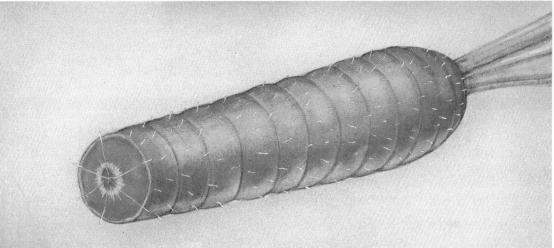

Here is a way to look at the thin, fine roots of a plant. Pull a weed with its roots. Look at the roots. Is the root a single root with small side branches like the carrot? Or is it a group of small roots?

Use a hand lens to look at the smaller roots. Look for tiny pieces of soil holding onto the roots. Water and minerals from the tiny pieces of soil can easily enter the smaller roots.

Plant roots have special parts called **root hairs.** Root hairs are very thin and grow near the tips of the smaller roots. Water and minerals soak easily through the thin root hairs.

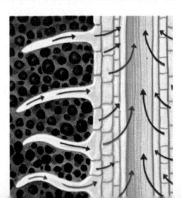

You can look at root hairs on some seedlings. You will need radish or corn seeds, damp paper toweling, a dish, plastic wrap, a dropper, red ink or red food coloring, and a hand lens.

Place the seeds on the damp paper in the dish. Cover the dish with plastic wrap. Keep the paper damp.

After a few days, the seeds become seedlings. With your hand lens look at the young roots on the seedlings. On which part of the root do you find root hairs? Describe what they look like. Now add a few drops of red ink or red food coloring to the wet toweling. Do the root hairs soak up the colored water?

Some of the water and minerals remain in the roots of the plant. But some keep right on going. They flow through thin tubes all the way up the stem and into the leaves.

Getting Water to the Leaves

The stem is the main food-carrying part of the plant. Stems have tubes that carry water and minerals from the roots to the leaves. Other tubes carry food from the leaves to other plant parts.

Here is a way to see how materials flow through a stem. You will need the stems and leaves of some celery and two different cut flowers. You also need some water, three glasses, food coloring, a dropper, and a knife.

Add a few drops of food coloring to each glass of water. With your teacher's help, make a fresh cut from the bottom of the stem. Put some stem pieces into each of the three glasses and leave them overnight. The next day, look at the leaves and stems. Describe what you see.

Carefully cut the stems in half crosswise. Look at the cut ends. Which places have more color from the food coloring? Now cut the stems lengthwise. Look at the stringy parts at the end of the stem. Do some of the strings have more color than others? The stringy parts of the stems are tubes. In what direction does the color in the tubes move? Water and minerals move up from the roots through these tubes.

Most stems have hundreds of thin tubes. Some plants have tubes that are scattered throughout their stems. Other plants have tubes that are found in a circle around the edge of their stems. Stems also support the plant. They hold up the flowers and leaves. Why do you think this is important?

Many different kinds of stems are found in green plants. The trunks of large trees such as oaks and maples are also stems. Some plants have long, thin stems that grow around other things. Other plants have stems that have tough covers and centers of soft material.

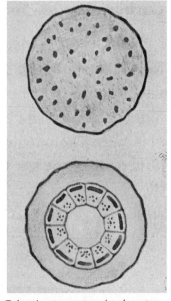

Tubes in stems carry food, water, and minerals.

Different kinds of stems

Carbon Dioxide for Photosynthesis

Besides water, plants also need carbon dioxide for photosynthesis. Plants get carbon dioxide from the air. Carbon dioxide enters the food-making part of the plant, the leaf, through tiny openings. The openings are found mostly on the underside of the leaves. This close-up view shows the tiny openings much larger than they really are.

Openings on underside of leaf

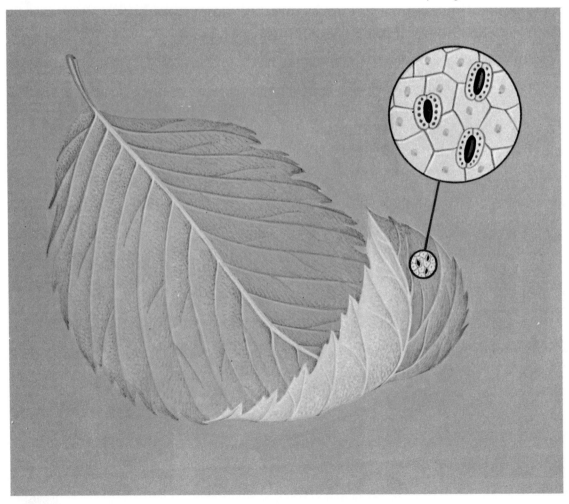

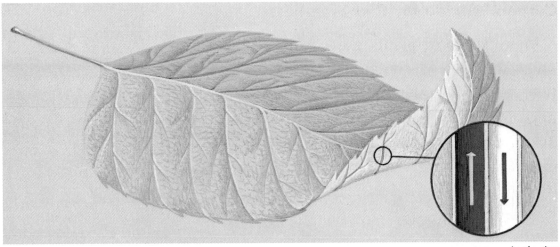

Leaf veins

If you look closely at a leaf, you will see lines that go through it. These lines are called **veins** [vaynz]. The veins help to hold up the leaf. The veins also contain little tubes. Some of these tubes carry water and minerals to the chlorophyll in the leaf. Other tubes in the veins carry the food made in the leaf down to the stem. The tubes in the stem then carry food to the branches of the plant. Finally, the food is carried to the root.

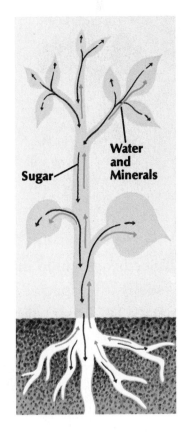

Some of the sugar that is made in the leaf is food for the growing leaf. The rest of it, mixed in water, goes through tubes to every part of the plant. Some of the sugar is changed into materials that the plant uses for building new parts. Some of it is not used to make new parts, but is stored instead. Some of the stored food is used by the plant when it is needed later. One place food is stored is in the seeds. This food will be used when the seeds grow into new plants.

Plants from Seeds

Many kinds of plants grow from seeds. You know that a seed contains a young plant. If a seed is put into the soil and has everything it needs, the plant inside will grow. It will become a grown plant like the one from which it came.

Variety of seeds

Seeds are made in a special part of the plant. Usually the special parts have pretty, colored **petals** [PEHT-lz] around them, but sometimes they are found in cones. In some plants the seed-making parts are tucked inside very tiny flowers. In other plants the parts are big enough to see easily. They are inside very large flowers.

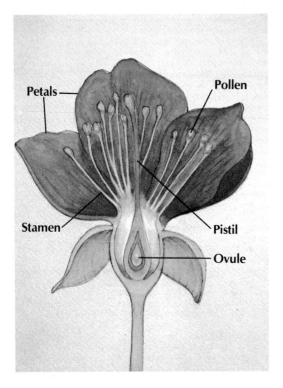

Petunia

In this flower you can see a part shaped like a vase with a long neck. This is called the **pistil** [PIHS-tl]. The pistils of different flowers look different. Down inside the pistil are very small beadlike parts called **ovules** [OH-vyoolz]. Ovules are the beginnings of seeds.

Most ovules cannot begin to grow and become plants until pollen reaches the pistil. The pollen is very close by. It is in the same flower as you see here. The pollen is found in knobs at the tips of long stems. Together, these knobs and stems are called **stamens** [STAY-muhnz]. Or pollen can also be found on stamens in another flower of the same kind. But this pollen cannot walk or fly. It must be carried.

Trumpet lily

You can look at the seed-making parts of a flower by cutting apart the flower. You will need a flower like the one in the picture. You will also need three straight pins, a hand lens, some white paper, and some tape.

Carefully look at your flower while it is whole. Make a drawing of it before you cut it apart. Name any parts that you know.

Lay the flower on a piece of white paper. How many petals does your flower have? Put the point of a pin where the petals seem to be joined together. Look at the picture. Pull the pin down toward the bottom of the flower. Do not press too hard. Press just hard enough for the pin to cut through the petals, but not through the whole flower.

Gladiolus flower

Pin fastened to Gladiolus pistil

Gladiolus stamens and pistil

Gladiolus stamens

Gladiolus ovary and ovules

Lift the cut petals and lay them flat, like the pages of a book. Use your other two pins to fasten the petals down. What do you see? Find the pistil. Find the stamens. Remove them carefully. Look at the knobs at the tips of the stamens. Touch one to a piece of white paper. The powder you see is the pollen grains.

Now you should be able to see the large bottom of the pistil more clearly. Gently run a straight pin down the side of it to open it. Place the hand lens above the flower so that you can see the opened part clearly. The small, skinny, beadlike parts are the ovules.

Keep a record of what you have learned by saving the parts of the flower. Lay some of the petals on one side of the paper. Fasten them with plastic tape. Lay the stamens on the paper and fasten them down. Do this with the rest of the flower. Label the parts.

How Pollen Is Carried

Some birds and insects carry pollen from the stamens to the pistil of the same flower. Or they carry pollen from the stamens of one flower to the pistil of another flower of the same kind. Pollen rubs onto their bodies as they sip the nectar deep inside the flower. Some pollen may drop onto the pistil of that flower, Or, when the bird or insect goes to the next flower, some pollen is brushed onto the pistil. In either case, a little tube begins to grow down the pistil from each pollen grain. The material in the pollen grain then flows through this tube and into an ovule.

Hummingbird

Honeybee

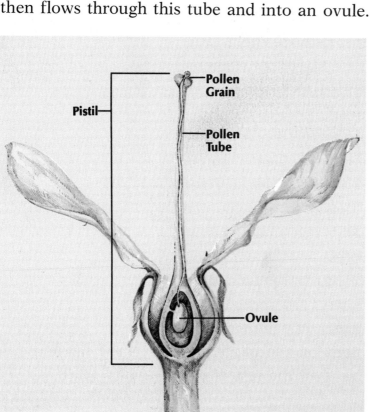

Together, ovules and pollen can change into seeds. The seeds contain young plants that can grow into big plants.

The colors and the sweet odors of flowers are useful to the plant, too. They attract insects and birds that carry pollen from flower to flower. Without pollen, most flowers could not make seeds.

Some plants have small flowers, without bright colors or pleasant odors. These flowers do not attract insects. Their pollen is usually carried by the wind.

Orange flower

Ponderosa pine

Larch

Japanese yew

Seeds Grow and Ripen

However, no matter how different flowers look or smell, they make seeds in the same way—out of ovules and pollen grains. A flower does not last very long. It dries up, usually leaving a few flower parts. If you look at the parts of a dried-up flower, you will see the ovules growing and ripening into seeds. The large bottom part of the pistil ripens, too. This part has the seeds and is called the **fruit.** The pictures below show how this takes place in some plants that we grow for food. Which parts of the pistil can you still see in the pictures?

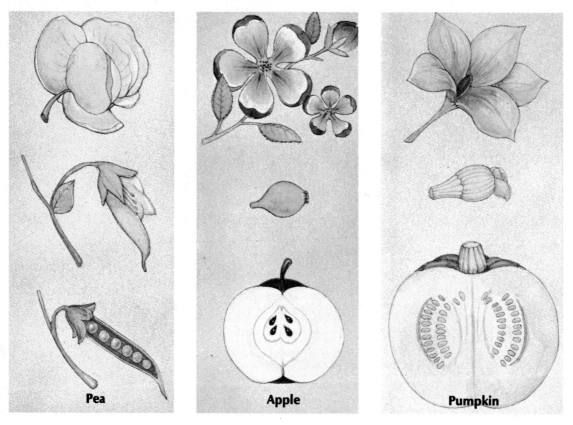

Pea   Apple   Pumpkin

Can you name these fruits? For each fruit can
you tell:

1. Which is the seed? Which is the ripened,
   bottom part of the pistil?
2. In which plants do we eat only the seeds?
3. In which plants do we not eat the seeds?
4. In which plants do we eat the whole fruit?

What Did You Learn?

- During photosynthesis, sunlight acts on chlorophyll in a leaf.
- Chlorophyll and light energy cause carbon dioxide to combine with water to make sugar and oxygen.
- Roots give support to plants, and take in water and minerals from the soil.
- Stems have tubes that carry water and minerals from the roots to the leaves, and food from the leaves to the rest of the plant.
- The leaves and other green parts of a plant make the food that feeds the whole plant.
- All flowering plants have seed-making parts: the ovules in the pistil and the pollen on the stamens.
- Seeds grow and ripen when the material in the pollen grows through the pistil and enters an ovule.
- The part of the pistil that surrounds the seeds is the fruit.

Career

Horticulturist

Do you have a garden? If you do, you are a **horticulturist** [HOHR-tuh-KUHL-chur-ihst].

People who grow fruits and vegetables are called horticulturists. They may also grow flowers and plants for office buildings and your home. They know how and when to start and take care of plants. Science has helped to improve the growing of plants. New materials have been made to help plants grow and to keep insects away. Now it is often possible to grow more than one crop in a season. It takes much training to learn the science of horticulture.

You may have seen special plants in stores, banks, and other buildings during holidays. Horticulturists use greenhouses to grow plants all year around. Some plan beautiful yards, gardens, and parks and ways to take care of them. Horticulturists try to grow bigger and better plants for everyone to enjoy.

TO THINK ABOUT AND DO

Number a piece of paper one through seven. Next to each number write the word from Column B that matches the group of words that describes it in Column A.

Column A

1. Green material that makes food in plants
2. Happens when light and chlorophyll cause carbon dioxide to combine with water to make sugar and oxygen
3. Part of a plant that gives support and takes in water and minerals from the soil
4. Part of a plant that contains tubes for carrying water and minerals to the leaves, and food from the leaves to the rest of the plant
5. Seed-making part in the pistil
6. Holds pollen at its tip
7. Part of the pistil that surrounds the seeds

Column B

stamen
fruit
stem
photosynthesis
root
ovule
chlorophyll

296

Copy each sentence on a piece of paper. Write **T** beside the sentences that are true and **F** beside those that are false. Rewrite any sentence that is false to make it true.

1. Without pollen, most flowers could not make seeds.
2. Plant stems contain root hairs through which water and minerals enter the plant.
3. The leaves and other green parts of a plant make food for the whole plant.
4. When the material in the pollen grows through the pistil and into an ovule, leaves begin to grow.

SOMETHING TO PUZZLE OVER

Try to answer this question. You may want to get some ideas from your classmates and materials from your teacher.

Why do farmers move beehives into fruit orchards in the spring?

ACTIVITY

You have a white flower and you want to change the color to blue. How would you do this? Try this with several flowers. Make each flower a different color. How does the color get to the flower?

The Earth's Resources

10

It's a great day for a long hike with some friends. You are eager to start on your way. You go up and down hills, over big rocks, and across streams. As the morning wears on, you begin to get tired. You are running out of energy. Finally, everyone agrees to stop for a rest and eat lunch.

Just sitting in the shade feels good. You would stay there all day if you could! After eating lunch and drinking some water, you feel your energy coming back. You are ready for the rest of the hike.

photo at left: Hiking along a mountain trail

The Earth: A Large Store

What are some of the things you would use on a long hike? Some things like food, water, and air, you would use just to stay alive. You would need other things, like special clothing and tools, to protect yourself and to have a safe hike. You find the matter that these things are made of all around you. In one way or another, they were all taken from the earth. The useful things that you take from the earth are called **resources** [REE-sohrs-uhz].

A large store is well stocked with many different things. The earth is something like a large store. Its atmosphere, water, and land are well stocked with many different resources. Some of the earth's resources are out in the open where everyone can see them. Resources such as water, air, soil, and living things can be found easily.

Colorado

Coal mine

But many of the earth's resources are hidden. Coal, natural gas, oil, and certain rocks and minerals are found beneath the surface of the earth. They are like the things that are kept in the back of a crowded storeroom. These resources are hard to find, and once found, it takes time to get them out.

Resources such as water, air, soil, and living things are returned to the earth after they are used. In a few days, months, or years, these resources are back in the earth's "store" ready to be used again. These resources are called **renewable** [rih-NOO-uh-buhl].

But resources like minerals, rocks, and fuels are not renewable at the rate at which we use them. There is only a certain amount of each of these resources. They can't be returned to the earth fast enough once they have been used.

Nearly everything that people use today comes from the earth's resources. Let's find out which of these resources are renewable and which of them are not.

Fuel from Green Plants

Long ago the weather in many places on the earth was hot and steamy for many years. It was something like a rainy tropical place today. There were many large swamps on the earth. The swamps were filled with green plants that lived and died in the warm sunlight. These plants took in carbon dioxide from the air and used the sun's energy to make food. When the green plants died and sank into the water, some energy remained stored in their materials. The swamp itself sank fast enough to keep the dead plants covered with water. New plants grew on top of the old ones.

Artist's view of a swamp long ago

For many thousands of years, the layers of dead plants piled up, thicker and thicker. Then the land began to sink much faster in some places. The swamps became lakes or seas. Through many years the dead plants became covered with sediments that were washed down by streams into the lakes or seas. The heat and pressure of the sediments changed the plant material into a partly finished **coal** called **lignite** [LIHG-nyt].

More heat and pressure on the layers of plant material turned it to a dull, black, crumbly coal. This soft coal is **bituminous** [buh-TOO-muh-nuhs] coal. When bituminous coal is heated, it burns slowly. As it burns, the coal gives off the energy that was stored in the plant material from which it was formed.

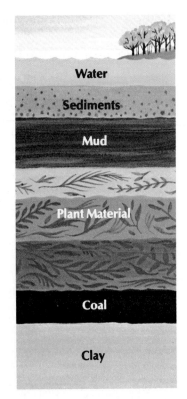

Water

Sediments

Mud

Plant Material

Coal

Clay

Lignite Coal   Bituminous Coal

Strip mine

Miners dig this ancient, stored-up sunlight out of the earth. Deposits of bituminous coal may be found on the surface or only a few meters beneath a covering of soil and rock. The miners often use huge machines that strip away the soil and rock covering. Then they can get the bituminous coal that is found beneath it.

In some places the sedimentary rock that has bituminous coal in it was pressed together and heated even more. These places were folded up or lifted to become mountain areas. As the sedimentary rock was changed to metamorphic rock, the coal within the rock was changed also. A hard, shiny coal called **anthracite** [AN-thruh-syt] was formed.

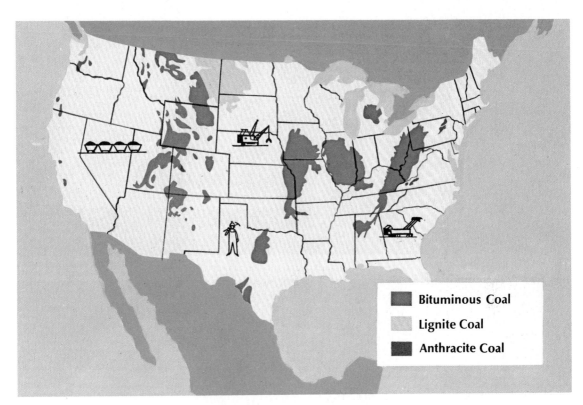

Anthracite coal burns with a steady flame and much less smoke than bituminous coal. In order to get the anthracite coal, miners must either blast the rock or dig tunnels into the rock that contains it. Some of these tunnels are thousands of meters deep.

Coal supplies the fuel used to make over half the electrical energy in the United States. This electrical energy is then used to power and heat homes, schools, and factories. Not all coal is used for fuel, though. You use coal every day, although you may not recognize it. Coal supplies the raw material for making dyes, perfume, plastics, nylons, and some medicines.

Coal-fired power plant

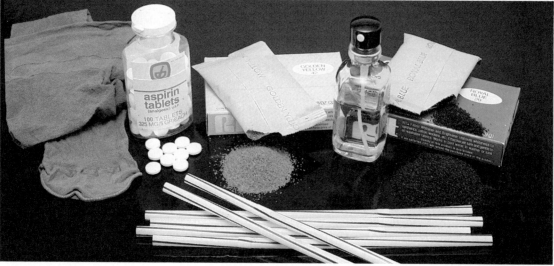

Things made from coal

How Oil Was Formed

Scientists believe that oil was made from many tiny plants, dead sea animals such as fish, and tiny sea organisms. All of these living things died and became covered with sediments. As the sediments became thicker and heavier, the pressure and heat may have melted and squeezed out the oil in these animals and plants. Then the oil gradually soaked into the sediments, which later became covered with more sediments.

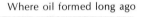

Where oil formed long ago

These things contain oil. This oil is not the same as the oil found underground.

Scientists have found that all animals and plants, no matter where they live or what their size, contain oil. You may have seen fat melting out of a chop or a piece of bacon. Or you may have heard about fish oils and duck and chicken fat.

Plants also have oil, although you do not usually notice it. Perhaps your parents use peanut oil, corn oil, and olive oil when they cook. If you look at the label on polishes, paints, and soaps, you may see some plant oils listed. Anything that has fat or oil in it leaves a shiny spot on paper. You may have seen such spots on a bag in which meat has been left.

Here are some ways to show that plants have oil. You need an orange or lemon peel, some brown paper, a peanut, some shelled nuts, and a brown paper bag.

Rub a peanut on the piece of brown paper. What happens? Does a peanut have oil in it?

Squeeze the orange or lemon peel over another part of the brown paper. Do you see shiny spots?

Put the shelled nuts into the brown bag. After a short time what do you notice? What does this tell you about the nuts?

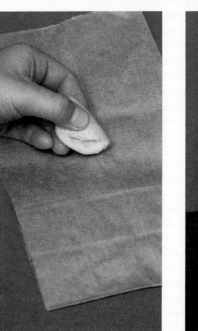

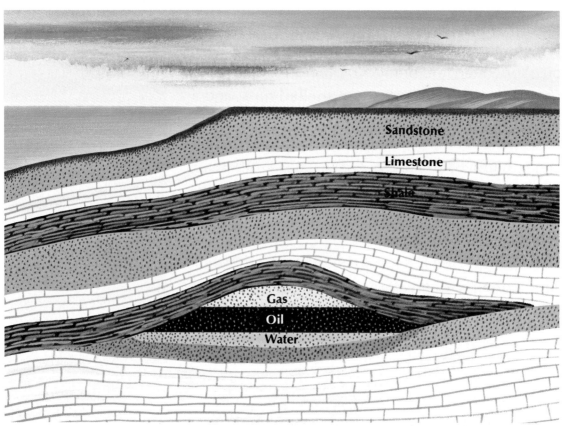

Oil is trapped when it reaches a nonporous layer.

Oil soaks very readily into sand. We say that sand is **porous** [POHR-uhs] because there are little holes or pores between the grains. Sandstone and shale, which are sedimentary rocks made from sand and clay, are fairly porous, too.

Oil that is found in these porous rocks is called **petroleum** [puh-TROH-lee-uhm], which means rock oil.

When oil was formed out of ancient plants and animals, it gradually soaked into the porous layers. It became trapped between the nonporous layers. The nonporous layers have kept the petroleum trapped for millions of years.

Here is a way to see why oil flows away from some places and collects in others. You will need some oil, several different kinds of small rocks of the same size, and a teaspoon of sand. You will also need some paper towels, an eyedropper, and a piece of unglazed clay or flowerpot.

Place your rock materials in a straight line on the paper towels. With the eye dropper, put one drop of oil on each. Watch the oil drops. Which materials absorb the oil quickly? Which do not? Try to see how many drops each material absorbs.

Labels on illustration: Sandstone, Limestone, Shale, Gas, Oil, Water

Holes must be drilled through layers of rock in order to reach gas and oil.

To bring up the petroleum, a hole is drilled through the layers of porous rock to the gas and oil. Sections of pipe are let down into the hole and fastened one above the other.

There is often a layer of gas above the oil. Sometimes there is enough of this natural gas to pipe off for use as a fuel.

Petroleum Fuel

The natural gas and oil deposits of the earth are valuable as fuel. In thousands of filling stations all over the world, people keep buying gasoline. They need millions of liters of gasoline every hour. Airplanes, ships, trucks, and trains keep burning up fuels—gasoline, kerosene, diesel oil, fuel oil.

Petroleum from natural gas and oil deposits is also valuable in making thousands of products. Scientists and engineers have found a way to separate the liquids and solids out of petroleum. They use this knowledge to separate wax, diesel oil, lubricating oils, kerosene, gasoline, and other materials out of petroleum. This separation is done in large factories called **refineries** [rih-FY-nuhr-eez].

Oil refinery

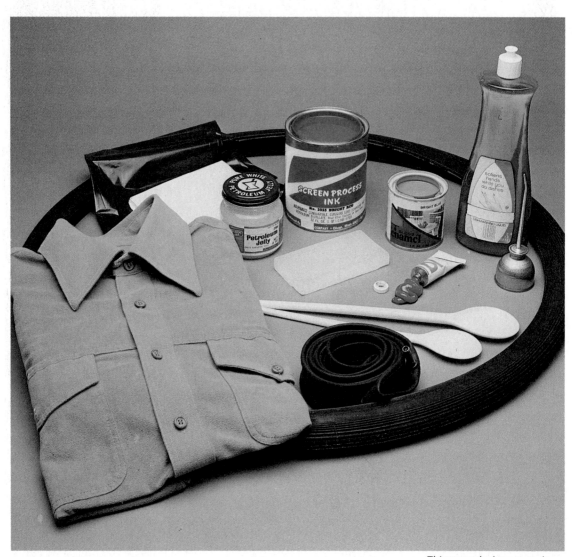

Things made from petroleum

Many things that we use every day are made from petroleum. The wax on the paper wrapper that keeps rolls and bread fresh comes from petroleum. Dry-cleaning liquids are made from petroleum, and so are the detergents used to wash dishes and clothes. Plastics, rubber tires, printing ink, some cloth fibers, and paint are just some of the thousands of petroleum products.

Gas and oil deposits in the earth were formed from plants and animals that lived and grew in the sunlight millions of years ago. Then, just as today, plants used the energy of sunlight in making food, and animals ate the plants. As in coal, the energy in oil and in natural gas is really the stored-up sunlight of millions of years ago.

By the end of the 21st century there may be little coal, oil, or natural gas left in the earth. These resources, which took millions of years to form, are rapidly being used up.

Oil refinery

Oil shales, Colorado

The fuels used by automobiles, buses, trucks, boats, trains, and airplanes come from oil. Our supplies of oil are being used up more quickly than new sources are being found. In order to make our supplies of oil last as long as possible, people are working together to find more oil. They are also trying to cut down on wasteful uses of oil.

New methods are being used to get the greatest amount of oil from the earth. Oil wells are being drilled deeper and new parts of the earth are being explored for deposits of oil. Another possible source of oil is oil shales. Oil shales are rocks that have large amounts of oil trapped in them. At present, however, getting oil from oil shales is very expensive.

Resources from Rocks and Minerals

No one knows for sure how ancient people first came to use rocks. Most likely they found shelter in rocky caves. They also used certain rocks for hunting and preparing their food. Over thousands of years people found many more ways to use igneous, sedimentary, and metamorphic rocks. How are these rocks being used? What are some other uses of rocks that you know about?

You know that rocks are made up of one or more minerals. While rocks themselves are a valuable resource, the minerals found in them are often even more valuable! When a mineral is found in large enough amounts so that it can be mined, the mineral is called an **ore** [ohr]. Most of the metals we use every day are taken from ores.

Ore deposits of gold, silver, iron, and other useful metals are found only in certain places. These minerals may have once been a part of the magma inside the earth. Magma, with many different mineral ores, moved along cracks in the earth's crust. As the ore minerals cooled, they separated out of the magma and filled the cracks or veins.

Gold in quartz vein

Gold mine

Some metals that have collected in veins are copper, silver, and gold. When the ore minerals collect in veins, it is often worth digging through rock layers to get at them. Where the mineral deposits are very valuable, mines are sometimes dug very deep.

Copper mine

Other ores are near the earth's surface. They can be taken from large open pits. Many metals are removed from ores by **smelting** [SMEHLT-ihng]. In smelting, the ore is heated with another material at very high temperatures. The high temperatures melt the mixture and the hot, liquidlike ore separates from the waste materials. The hot, liquidlike ore is removed and refined further, if necessary.

Smelting of ore

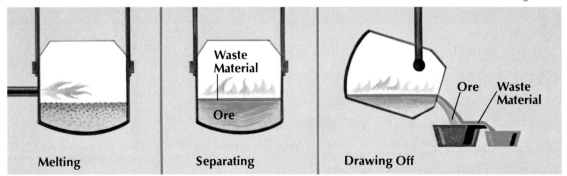

Melting   Separating   Drawing Off

320

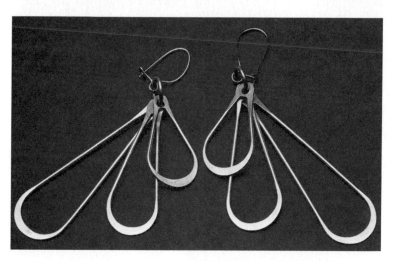

The metals taken from these ores are used in some of the ways that you see here. Large amounts of metals are brought into the United States every year. This is because we use more metals than can be mined in the United States. Just as fuels are not renewable, the ores from which we get these metals are not renewable. When the ores are used up, we shall have no choice but to use plastics, wood, and other materials instead of metals. We must also keep in mind, however, that plastics are made from oil. This resource is rapidly being used up.

Living Resources

The earth has living resources as well as nonliving resources. But unlike nonliving resources, living resources are replaced even as they are being used. That is why they are renewable.

All plants and animals pass through different stages as they grow. The time from the beginning of a living thing's first stage of growth to the end of its last stage of growth is a **life cycle** [lyf SY-kuhl]. Unless something happens to change a life cycle, there will always be living things in a population who are at different stages of growth. This means that while some in a population are growing older, others are just beginning their life cycle.

Life cycle of ponderosa pines

While some plants grow in just a few months, other plants must grow for several years before they are ready to be harvested. For example, in many places, pine tree forests are grown as crops. Seeds are gathered from those trees that have the most rapid and healthy growth. Young pines grown from these seeds are then planted in the forests. They replace those trees that were cut down after they grew to a certain size. The trees that were cut down are used for lumber, fuel, making paper, and in many other products. It isn't long before the young pine trees reach the right size for harvesting. Before they are cut down, some of their seeds are collected. The young pines grown from these seeds will replace the parent plants in the forest once again.

Hereford cattle

Cattle are a valuable renewable resource also. You eat the meat of cattle as roast beef, veal, hamburger, and hot dogs. You drink cow's milk, and you eat milk after it has been made into cheese, butter, and ice cream. Cattle give you leather for your shoes and also materials for the making of medicines, soap, and glue.

Cattle that make large amounts of milk or high-grade beef are mated when they are between 15 and 27 months old. The cows usually have one calf every year. The parent cattle are usually sold when they are a few years old. By that time, their young cows will be having calves that replace them. Since cattle have a short life cycle, new ones are always taking the place of those that were used.

Using Resources Wisely

The people who first settled in America found their new home had many resources. Rich soil, fresh water, forests, minerals, and animals were everywhere. But as the population increased, rich soils were used up and farmlands were worn out. Great forests were cut down. Huge scars were left in the earth as the minerals were mined. Beautiful rivers became polluted. Many wild animals were killed, some for food but most for their hides or other parts. Gradually, because Americans were not careful, they used up large amounts of these resources.

What resources are found here?

The population of the United States is expected to be more than 300 million by the year 2000. Not only is our population growing, but the amount of resources each person uses is growing. If we want to keep using some of these resources, we must use what remains of them more carefully. We must **conserve** [kuhn-SURV] our resources—use them wisely.

A way for people to conserve living resources is to not use them at a rate that is faster than the rate at which they are replaced. What resource is being renewed here? We must be careful not to turn a renewable resource into one that can't be replaced.

Stocking a pond

Resources such as oil, coal, natural gas, and ores can only be used once. They must be conserved. Some materials that are made from resources can be used more than once, or **recycled** [ree-SY-kuhld]. Metal, paper, and glass are materials that can be recycled. What are some materials you know of that can be recycled?

Aluminum cans are melted down and made into ingots.

When ores such as copper and aluminum are recycled, less ore needs to be taken from the earth. Every bit of mineral ore that is melted down and used again saves us from taking more from the earth's "store." When paper is recycled, fewer trees need to be cut down to make paper and cardboard boxes. It takes energy to mine the sand that makes glass. When old glass is melted and made into bottles, fuel is conserved. Otherwise, the fuel would have been used to mine more sand to make new glass.

327

People can also conserve resources by using less of them. When many people travel together in one car, bus, or train, less gasoline is used than if each person traveled alone. When people keep the temperature of their homes at 20 °C, they use less fuel than if they kept the temperature at 23 °C.

People can't get minerals and fuels out of the earth without making changes in its surface. The layer of soil and rock that covers the resources is removed during mining. Since the soil is mixed with other materials and put into piles, the land can't be used any more. But now people can rebuild the land and plant trees or crops on it. In this way, the land that was once mined can now be used again.

This land was once a strip mine.

Another way people can conserve resources is to use resources that are plentiful. They should use these resources instead of those that are in short supply. For example, clothing can be made either from living things or from fuels. Cotton, wool, and silk clothing are made from living things that have short life cycles. Since these resources are renewable, people will be able to get cotton, wool, and silk even after coal and petroleum are used up. So, making clothing from living things helps to conserve the fuels.

Removing wool from sheep

Perhaps we should look closely at nature and copy what happens there. The rose that blooms today could have been made of last year's crumbled leaves and this morning's dew. The resources in that rose have perhaps spent time in a seashell, a wheel, a butterfly, and a hawk. How old is this morning's rose? It is as new as a raindrop, as old as the hills. Since each bit of the rose is made from a resource that has been recycled, the rose is forever a part of the world!

What Did You Learn?

- All the useful things that are in and around the earth are called resources.
- Resources are renewable only if they can be replaced as they are used.
- Over millions of years coal was formed when layers of green plants came under the heat and pressure of the sediments that covered them.
- When layers of dead sea plants and animals were squeezed by the heat and pressure of sediments, oil was formed.
- Petroleum, or oil that is found in porous rocks, supplies people with many different fuels and other things that they use daily.
- An ore is a mineral from which a useful material can be removed.
- Living things are renewable because they have fairly short life cycles.
- People can conserve resources by recycling, by using only as many living things as their life cycles can replace, by using resources that are plentiful, and by trying not to waste resources.

Biography

Carol Gardipe (1935–   )

Minerals, oil, natural gas, and coal are some of the resources found in or on the earth. Geologists explore the earth for these resources and others that supply energy.

Carol Gardipe is a geologist who gathers information on offshore drilling. She gives information about where natural gas and oil may be found to people all over the world. She does this work for the National Oceanic and Atmospheric Administration (NOAA).

Carol is an American Indian from Maine. As a child, she spent many hours outdoors with her father. He was a guide, woodsman, hunter, and trapper. He was also an earth science teacher. Very early in her life Carol learned about trees, plants, stars, and seasons. She learned to track animals, to fish, and to travel in the woods or on water. Becoming a geologist was a way for Carol to spend time outdoors and study the earth.

Carol Gardipe has helped many Indians by training them in science and engineering. She hopes one day to help other Indians by studying the resources on the lands they own.

TO THINK ABOUT AND DO

On a piece of paper, copy the spaces and numbers of the puzzle. Then find a science word that goes with each clue and has the correct number of letters to fit the spaces.

Across

1. rock oil
3. hard, shiny coal
5. mineral found in amounts large enough to be mined
7. useful things that can be taken from the earth

Down

2. resource formed in ancient swamps and seas
4. places where ores can be removed from the earth
6. soft coal
8. way to remove metals from ores
9. resource made of dead plants and animals under pressure

334

Copy the sentences on a piece of paper. Complete the sentences with a science word from this chapter.

1. When layers of dead green plants came under heat and pressure for millions of years, _____ was formed.

2. Oil that is found in porous rock is called _____.

3. A mineral from which a useful material can be removed is a(n) _____.

4. When layers of dead sea plants and animals were squeezed together by heat and pressure, _____ was formed.

5. Resources such as cattle and trees that can be used and replaced are _____.

6. When we use materials over again to conserve resources, we _____ the materials.

Use books from your classroom or library to help you answer one of these questions.

1. How is coal used to make dyes, perfumes, and medicines?

2. What is strip mining? How can this kind of mining sometimes harm the land?

3. What are the different ways that people can conserve fuels?

Some of the science words used in this book may be new to you. Heath Science helps you to pronounce many of these new words.

These new science words are shown in darker print. These words are followed by a guide which shows you how to pronounce them.

Examples:

leaf [leef]
energy [EHN-ur-gee]
lava [LAH-vuh]

The pronunciation guide shows you how each syllable of the word should sound. The syllable in capital letters is the one that has the accent.

The chart below is used with permission from *The World Book Encyclopedia*. The first column shows examples of dictionary pronunciations. The second column shows how the sounds are written. The third column shows examples of words which contain each of the sounds, followed by the pronunciation guides.

Dictionary Pronunciation		How the Sound Is Written	Example	
a	h*a*t, m*a*p	a	ANIMAL	AN-uh-muhl
ā	*a*ge, f*a*ce	ay	SPACE	spays
â	c*a*re, *ai*r	ai	HAIR	hair
ä	f*a*ther, f*a*r	ah	LARGE	lahrj
ch	*ch*ild, mu*ch*	ch	CHEW	choo
e	l*e*t, b*e*st	eh	ENERGY	EHN-ur-gee
ē	*e*qual, s*ee* machi*ne*, cit*y*	ee	LEAF	leef
ėr	t*er*m, l*ear*n, s*ir*, w*or*k	ur	EARTHWORMS	URTH-wurms
i	*i*t, p*i*n	ih	SYSTEM	SIHS-tuhm
ī	*i*ce, f*i*ve	eye	IODINE	EYE-uh-dyn
k	*c*oat, loo*k*	k	CORN	kohrn
o	h*o*t, r*o*ck	ah	ROCK	rahk
ō	*o*pen, g*o* gr*ow*	oh	MOLDS	mohldz
ô	*o*rder, *a*ll	aw	FALL	fawl
oi	*oi*l, v*oi*ce	oy	POISON	POY-zuhn
ou	h*ou*se, *ou*t	ow	FOUNTAIN	FOWN-tuhn
s	*s*ay, ni*c*e	s	SOIL	soyl
sh	*sh*e, aboli*t*ion	sh	MOTION	MOH-shuhn
u	c*u*p, b*u*tter, fl*oo*d	uh	BULB	buhlb
			BLOOD	bluhd
u̇	f*u*ll, p*u*t, w*oo*d	u	WOOL	wul
ü	r*u*le, m*o*ve, f*oo*d	oo	DEW	doo
zh	plea*s*ure	zh	EROSION	ih-ROH-zhuhn
ə	*a*bout, am*e*ba	uh	LAVA	LAH-vuh
	tak*e*n, purp*le*	uh	FIDDLE	FIHD-uhl
	penc*i*l	uh	CYCLE	SY-kuhl
	lem*o*n	uh	CARBON	KAHR-buhn
	circ*u*s	uh	MUSCLES	MUHS-uhlz
	curt*ai*n	uh	MOUNTAIN	MOWN-tuhn
	sec*t*ion	uh	DIGESTION	dy-JEHS-chuhn

Abdomen [AB-duh-muhn]: part of the body of an insect, 5

Acid rain, 173

Adult, the final stage of animal growth, 14, 15, 17, 18, 36

Air, carbon dioxide for plants from, 284; dirty, 172–173; gases in, 144, 174; materials for food from, 277, 278; as matter, 142–143; movement of, 168–171; as a resource, 300; water vapor in, 144. *See also* Atmosphere

Air molecules, and temperature, 157–158, 164–166, 168, 174

Air pressure [ehr PREHSH-uhr]: the force that causes air molecules to press in all directions, 149, 150–154, 174; in atmosphere, 156; doing work with, 153, 155–156, 174; and drinking with straws, 154; studying changes in, 159; and temperature, 157–158, 174

Animals, fossil, 261, 263; oil from, 315, 332; plants needed by, 34

Antennae [an-TEHN-ee]: special head parts of insects, 10, 19, 36

Anthracite [AN-thruh-syt]: hard, shiny coal formed in metamorphic rock, 305

Ants, 25, 30–31

Asteroids [AS-tuh-roydz]: planet-like objects orbiting the sun between Mars and Jupiter, 182, 183, 238; belt, 218

Atmosphere [AT-muhs-fihr]: the mixture of gases surrounding a planet, 141, 174; heating, 164–167, 174; of Jupiter, 221; keeping it clean, 172–173, 174; of Mercury, 211; of moon, 209; pressure of air in, 156; of Saturn, 225, 226. *See also* Air

Atoms [AT-uhmz]: tiny particles making up all matter, 115, 118–119, 136; molecules made from, 119; movement of, 118, 119

Axle [AK-suhl]: 60, 64–66

Backbone, 82

Basalt [buh-SAWLT]: an igneous rock formed from slow-cooling lava, 253. *See also* Obsidian

Bees, 25, 26–29

Birds, insects as food for, 24, 33; killed by poisons, 33; pollen carriers, 290, 291

Bituminous [buh-TOO-muh-nuhs]: soft, slow-burning coal found near surface of the earth, 303–304

Blood, made in bones, 88, 104; moved by action of heart, 102–103

Body, air pressure and, 150–151; skeleton framework for, 79, 104

Bones, 79; of arms and legs, 85; and cartilage, 93–94, 97, 104; fossil, 261; growth of, 83, 84; of head, 80; joints of, 89; minerals of, 86, 104; and muscles, 98–101; repair of, 87; ribs, 95

Breathing, dirty air, 197; movement of ribs during, 95; oxygen and carbon dioxide in, 146–147

Butterfly, 14, 23

Carbon dioxide [KAHR-buhn-dy-AHK-syd]: a gas in the atmosphere that is important for life on Earth, 144, 148; and breathing, 146–147; important use for, 148; on Mars, 215; needed for life on earth, 146; and photosynthesis, 284, 294; used by plants to make food, 278, 294, 302; on Venus, 212–213

Cartilage [KARH-tl-ihj]: a material that protects the ends of bones, 93–94, 97, 104; in nose, throat, and ears, 96

Chlorophyll [KLOHR-uh-fihl]: green food-making material in leaves of plants, 277–278, 285, 295

Clouds, and atmosphere, 141; on Jupiter, 221; around Uranus, 227; on Venus, 212; and water vapor, 148

Coal, anthracite, 305; being used up, 315; bituminous, 303, 304, 305; conserving, 327; electrical energy from, 306; as fuel, 303, 305–306; harmful matter from, 172; made from dead plants, 303, 332; as resource, 301; as sedimentary rock, 258

Color, of flowers, 291; of insects, 23, 24, 36

Comet [KAHM-it]: an orbiting body of rock, gases, and ice that sweeps through the solar system, 228, 238

Compressed air [kuhm-PREHST ehr]: air that has been pressed into a smaller space, 155, 156

Conserve [kuhn-SURV]: to use carefully and wisely, living resources, 326; land and soil, 329; by not wasting, 328, 332; by recycling, 327

Copernicus [kuh-PUR-nuh-kuhs], 203

Cotton, clothing from, 330; and insect pests, 35

Craters [KRAY-tuhrz]: bowl-shaped holes on the surface of a moon or planet, of moon, 209; of Mercury, 210; on Mars, 215, 238

Crystals [KRIHS-tlz]: a mineral form that results when atoms take on a certain pattern, 250–251; cooling and size of, 253, 254–255, 270

Dinosaur [DY-nuh-sawr]: one kind of prehistoric animal, 261

Drones [drohnz]: male bees, 29

Earth, in solar system, 182, 200–201, 208, 219, 238

Eggs, of bees, 29; of insects, 15, 18, 19, 36

Energy, electrical, 306; from green plants, 276; heat, 123, 125, 127, 130–131, 136; in natural gas and oil, 315; and oxygen, 144–145; from plants, 302; from sun, 212, 227, 228, 230, 238, 275–276, 294, 302

Equator [i-KWAY-tuhr]: an imaginary line on the surface of the earth that goes around its center, 195

Evaporation [ih-vap-uh-RAY-shuhn]: a liquid changing to a gas, 125; and comets, 228; studying, 126; and using matter, 134, 136

Eyes, of insects, 12–13, 36

Flowers, and bees, 25–27, 33; fruit from, 292, 294; parts of, 287; pollen of, 290–291; and seed-making, 286–287, 294; studying seed-making parts of, 288–289

Food, for bees, 25–27; insects as, 24; and plants, 276–279, 285, 294; and sun's energy, 275

Force [fohrs]: a push or pull that can cause something to move, 43, 74; acting on molecules, 120, 122; air pressure as, 150; of compressed air, 155; gravitation as, 113–114, 136; and inclined plane, 53, 54, 55; and levers, 47–51; measuring, 45; between molecules, 122; and pulleys, 62, 63; and screws, uses of, 44–46

Fossils [FAHS-uhlz]: remains of animals and plants that have been changed to rock, 261, 263; making, 262; in sediments, 270

Freezing [FREE-zihng]: changing the form of matter from a liquid to a solid; and heat energy, 131; and using matter, 134, 136

Friction [FRIHK-shuhn]: the force needed to move one surface over another surface, 67, 74; cartilage helps reduce, 93, 94, 97, 104; lubrication and, 70, 71; using, 72–73, 74

Fruit, part of the pistil that surrounds the seed, 294; from flowers, 292, 293

Fuels, clothes from, 330; mining, 329; natural gas, 312, 313; petroleum, 313, 316, 332; saved by recycling, 327; trees as, 323

Fulcrum [FUHL-kruhm]: the turning point about which a lever moves, 47–51

Gases, matter in a form that can fill any space, 125; in atmosphere, 144, 148, 149, 174; in comets, 228; and heat energy, 130; matter as, 132–133, 136; molecules of, 127–128; natural, 312, 313; and odors, 129; of Saturn, 182, 225; of Uranus, 182, 227; water becoming, 125–127; and volcanoes, 247

Geologists [jee-AHL-uh-jihsts], 271

Globe [glohb]: a model of the earth, 191, 195

Gneiss [nys]: a metamorphic rock made of the same minerals as granite, 266

Granite [GRAN-iht]: a kind of igneous rock made up of mineral crystals, 250; made below the earth's surface, 253; and metamorphic rock formation, 266

Grasshopper, 5

Gravitation [grav-uh-TAY-shun]: the force with which all things pull on one another's mass, 113–114, 136; and atmosphere, 141, 149; and discovery of Neptune, 229; on Jupiter, 223; and Pluto, 230; of Saturn, 225; in solar system, 185–186, 187; studying, 186; of sun, 184, 202

Great Red Spot, 222, 238

Head parts, of insects, 5, 36

Heat, and formation of coal, 303, 305; and formation of oil, 307, 332; and metamorphic rock formation, 265, 266–267, 270; and rock cycle, 268, 269; for smelting ores, 320. *See also* Temperature

Heat energy, changing forms of matter with, 123, 125, 127, 130–131; and movement of molecules, 122, 125, 127, 136; from sun, 211

Hornets, 25

Horticulturist [HOHR-tuh-KUHL-chur-ihst], 295

Hurricane [HUR-uh-kayn]: a large storm, 222

Hydrogen [HY-druh-juhn]: one kind of atom found in water, 119

Igneous [IHG-nee-uhs] rocks: rocks formed from hot magma, 248; basalt as, 253–254; changing, 165; granite, 250, 253; from magma, 270; minerals in, 249–250, 252, 253; obsidian, 253; and rock cycle, 268; using, 317

Inclined plane [ihn-KLYND playn]: a kind of machine made of a sloping board with one end higher than the other end, 52–55

Insects, body parts of, 4–13, 36; color, shape, and markings of, 23, 24, 36; fossil, 261; glowing, 22, 36; growth stages of, 14–18, 36; pests, 32–35, 36; pollen-carrying, 25–27, 33, 290, 291; sense of hearing in, 21; sense of smell, 19–20, 21; social, 25–31, 36

Joint [joynt]: place where bones come together that allows the skeleton to move, 89; ball and socket, 91; cartilage in, 93–94, 104; hinge, 90; sliding, 92

Jupiter [JOO-puh-tuhr]: the largest planet and fifth in the solar system, 182, 218–223

La Brea [lah-BRAY-uh]: a tar pit in California where prehistoric animals were caught and preserved, 163

Land, cooling, 162–163; heating, 160–162, 174; as a resource, 300, 329. *See also* Soil

Larva [LAHR-vuh]: a worm-like stage in insect growth, 15, 16, 17, 36

Lava [LAV-uh]: hot liquid rock that escapes at the surface of the earth, 247, 253

Layers, coal forming, 303, 332; of natural gas, 312; of sediments, 256

Leaves, getting water to, 282–283; food made by, 276–278, 279; fossil, 261; openings for carbon dioxide in, 284; photosynthesis in, 278, 294; veins in, 285

Legs, of insects, 4, 7, 36

Lens, using, 9, 116, 117

Lever [LEHV-uhr]: a kind of machine, 47–51, 74

Life cycle [LYF SY-kuhl]: the time from the beginning of a living thing's first stage of growth to the end of its last stage of growth, 322; of cattle, 324; of plants, 323; and renewable resources, 330, 332

Ligaments [LIGH-uh-muhnts]: long tough cords that tie bones together at joints, 96, 97, 104

Light, and photosynthesis, 278

Light energy, 211, 294. *See also* Energy

Lignite [LIHG-nyt]: plant material that has changed into partly finished coal, 303

Limestone [LYM-stohn]: a sedimentary rock, 258; fossils found in, 263; marble made from, 265

Liquid [LIHK-wihd]: matter in a form that does not keep its shape, but fits that of a container, crystals from, 251; and heat energy, 130–131; matter as, 132–133, 136; molecules of, 122–124, 130; rocks as, 246–247

Lubrication [loo-bruh-KAY-shuhn]: getting rid of friction by using a material that makes surfaces slippery, 70, 71, 74; in joints, 97

Machine [muh-SHEEN]: a thing that enables people to use less force to do more work; inclined plane, 52–55, 74; lever, 47–51, 74; pulleys, 60–63, 74; screws, 56–57, 74; and using force, 46; wedges, 58–59, 74; wheel and axle, 64–66, 74

Magma [MAG-muh]: thick melted rock below the earth's surface, 246–247; crystal formation in, 254–255; igneous rock from, 270; and metamorphic rock, 267; minerals in, 250, 318; and rock cycle, 268; rocks formed from, 248, 252–255

Marble, 265

Marrow [MAR-oh]: material inside bone that makes blood, 88, 104

Mars [Mahrz]: the fourth planet of the solar system, 182, 214–218, 219, 238; seasons on, 198; studying movement of, 200–201

Mass [mas]: the amount of matter in a thing, 112, 136; of air, 149, 157–158; force of gravitation on, 114; of Jupiter, 220

Materials, for plant life, 277–281, 284–285

Matter [MAT-uhr]: what everything in the world is made of, 111, 136; air as, 142–143; atoms and molecules of, 115, 117–121, 130; effects of heat energy on, 123, 125; gases, 125; harmful, 172–173; liquid, 122–124; solid, 120, 121; takes up space and has mass, 112; using and changing, 134–135

Melting, changing the form of matter from a solid to a liquid; water, 122; and heat energy, 123, 131; and using matter, 134, 136

Mercury [MUR-kyuh-ree]: the planet in the solar system that is closest to the sun, 182, 210–211, 238; studying movement of, 201

Metals, on Mercury, 211; ore deposits of, 318–319; recycling, 327; use of, 321

Metamorphic [meht-uh-MOHR-fihk] rocks: rocks that have been changed by intense heat and pressure, 265; anthracite coal from, 305; formation of, 270; gneiss, 266; marble, 265; and rock cycle, 268; slate, 266; using, 317

Minerals [MIHN-uhr-uhlz]: of bone, 86, 104; conserving, 327; crystals of, 250–251, 253–255, 270; in igneous rocks, 249; in magma, 252–253; mining, 329; ores, 318, 332; for plants, 278, 279, 280, 282–283, 285; as a resource, 301, 317, 325; rocks made of, 270; and sedimentary rocks, 256

Model, of Earth, 193, 195; of solar system, 232–235

Moist [moyst] air: air that contains water vapor, 156

Molecules [MAHL-uh-kyoolz]: tiny particles of matter made up of atoms that have come together in a certain way, 119, 136; of air, 150, 152, 153, 157–158, 164–167, 174; effects of sunlight on, 164–165; effects of temperature on, 166; of gases, 127–128; and heat energy, 130–131, 136; of liquids, 122–124, 127; movements of, 120, 122, 123, 124, 125, 134; of solids, 120, 121, 124; of water, 119–120

Moons, Earth's, 209; of Jupiter, 220, 223; of Mars, 217; of Neptune, 229, 230; revolving around planets, 209, 238; of Saturn, 226

Mouth parts, of insects, 11, 36

Muscles [MUHS-uhlz]: and breathing, 94–95; healthy, 101; heart, 102–103; moving bones, 98; in stomach and intestine, 102; in a system, 184; working in pairs, 99–100, 104

Natural gas, being used up, 315; conserving, 327; a form of stored-up sunlight, 315; as fuel, 312, 313; harmful matter from, 172; as a resource, 301

Navigator [NAV-uh-gay-tuhr], 175

Nectar [NEHK-tuhr]: sweet liquid from flowers that is made into honey by bees, 25–27, 290

Neptune [NEHP-toon]: the eighth planet in the solar system, 182, 229, 230, 238

Newton [NOOT-n]: a unit for measuring force, 45

Nitrogen [NY-truh-juhn]: a gas that makes up about four-fifths of the earth's atmosphere, 144, 148

Nymph [nimf]: one of the stages of insect growth, 18, 36

Obsidian [awb-SIHD-ee-uhn]: a rock formed by the rapid cooling of lava, 253

Odors, of flowers, 291; insects and, 19, 21; molecules of gases and, 128–129

Oil, being used up, 315; conserving, 327; a form of stored-up sunlight, 315; harmful matter from, 314, 321; a resource, 301; from sediments, 307, 308–309, 332; wasting, 316. *See also* Petroleum

Oil shales, 316

Orbit [OHR-biht]: a path in which a planet travels around the sun, 185, 202, 238; of asteroids, 219; of Earth, 196; of Jupiter, 218, 228; of Mars, 218; of Pluto, 230; of Uranus, 227, 229. *See also* Revolution

Ore [ohr]: a mineral from which a useful material can be removed, 318, 319, 332;

being used up, 315; conserving, 327; near the earth's surface, 320

Ovules [OH-vyoolz]: small bead-like parts of flowers that are the beginning of seeds, 287, 289; and making seeds, 292, 294

Oxygen [AHK-suh-juhn]: a gas that makes up about one-fifth of the atmosphere, 144; in atmosphere, 148; atoms of, 119; and breathing, 146–147; how we get energy from, 145; made by plants, 278, 294; water made of, 119

Pests, insect, 32–35, 36

Petals [PEHT-lz]: the colored leaves around the seed-making parts of plants, 286

Petrify [PEHT-ruh-fy]: to become solid rock, 264

Petroleum [puh-TROH-lee-uhm]: oil formed from ancient plants and animals that is stored in rocks, 310, 332; fuels from, 313; products of, 313–314; recovering, 312. *See also* Oil

Photosynthesis [foh-toh-SIHN-thuh-sihs]: green plants make sugar in the presence of light, 278, 279, 294; carbon dioxide for, 284

Pistil [PIHS-tl]: a part of a flower containing the ovules, 287, 289, 294; becomes fruit, 292; and pollen, 290

Planet [PLAN-iht]: a body in the solar system that revolves around the sun in an orbit, 182, 202; changing positions of, 199–202; gravitation and, 185; revolutions of, 185–189; rotation of, 190–192, 202, 211, 213, 226; of solar system, 182–184; studying, 207; sun's light reflected by, 181

Plants, carbon dioxide used by, 146, 284; coal from, 332; effects of dirty air on, 173; food made in, 276–279; fossil, 261, 263, 270; fuels from, 302–303; need for animals, 34; oil from, 308–309; oxygen made by, 146; petroleum made from, 307, 315; as renewable resource, 323; in sediments, 270; seeds of, 286–291; sunlight and, 275–278, 294

Plastics, made from coal, 306; made from oil, 314, 321

Pluto [PLOO-toh]: the outermost planet in the solar system, 182, 230–231, 238

Poison, for insect pests, 32–35, 36

Poles, of Earth, 195, 196, 197; of Mars, 198, 215, 217, 238; of Uranus, 227

Pollen [PAHL-uhn]: powder found on the stamens of flowers needed to make seeds, and bees, 25–27, 33; how it is carried, 290–291; and making seeds, 287, 292, 294

Pollution, harmful matter in the water, land, or air; in atmosphere, 172–173; of water, 325; in soil, 32–35, 36

Population, and resources, 326

Porous [POHR-uhs]: having little holes, or pores, that allow liquids to pass through, 310, 312

Pressure, and coal formation, 303, 305; and metamorphic rock formation, 265, 266, 267, 270; and oil formation, 307, 332; and rock cycle, 268, 269; and sedimentary rock formation, 247, 256

Pulley [PUHL-ee]: a kind of machine that uses wheel(s) and rope(s), 60–63; fixed, 60, 61; movable, 61–63; using, 62–63

Pupa [PYOO-puh]: the third of four stages in insect growth, 15, 17, 36

Ramp, an inclined plane, 54

Recycling [ree-SY-kling]: using a material more than once, and conserving resources, 332; in nature, 331

Refineries [rih-FY-nuhr-eez]: factories for separating solids, liquids, fuels, and other materials in petroleum, 313

Renewable [rih-NOO-uh-buhl] resources: resources that can be replaced as they are used, 301, 332; conserving, 326; living resources as, 322–324; using to save fuels, 330

Resources [REE-sohrs-uhz]: the useful things in and around the earth, 332; air

as, 300; being used up, 315–316; kinds of, 301; land and soil as, 300, 325, 329; living, 322–324; nature's use of, 331; using wisely, 325–331, 332; water as, 300, 325

Revolution [rehv-uh-LOO-shuhn]: one complete trip around the sun, 187, 188–189, 202, 226; of moons, 209

Ribs [rihbz]: the bones in the chest that are shaped like a cage, 81; movement of, 95

Rings, of Jupiter, 220; of Saturn, 224–225

Rock cycle [rahk SY-kuhl]: the building up and wearing away of rocks over millions of years, 268–269, 270

Rocks, in comets, 228; formation of, 245; igneous, 165, 247, 248–250, 252–255, 268, 270, 317; on Mercury, 211; metamorphic, 265–267, 268, 269, 270, 305, 317; porous, 332; resources from, 301, 317; sedimentary, 256–264, 266, 270, 310

Root hairs, of plants, 280

Roots, and food making, 279, 280, 281, 282, 294; insect eggs on, 19

Rotation [roh-TAY-shuhn]: the spinning movement of the earth and other planets, 190, 202; causing day and night, 191–192; of Mercury, 211; of Saturn, 226; of Venus, 213

Sandstone [SAND-stohn]: a soft sedimentary rock formed from minerals and sand, 263; fossils found in, 263; porousness of, 310

Saturn [SAT-uhrn]: the sixth planet in the solar system, 182, 223–226, 238

Scales [skaylz]: 45, 48, 53, 55, 62, 114

Scientists, 21, 207, 209, 217, 224, 264, 307, 308

Screws [skrooz]: a kind of machine, 56–57, 74

Seasons, Earth's, 193–198, 202; on Mars, 216; on other planets, 198

Sedimentary [sehd-uh-MEHN-tuhr-ee] rocks: rocks formed from layers of broken rock, minerals, and dead animals and plants; changing, 265; coal as, 258,

303, 305; formation of, 256, 257, 270; fossils in, 261; land and, 260; learning about the past from, 261–264; limestone as, 258; making, 259; and petroleum, 310, 322; and rock cycle, 268, 269; sandstone as, 263; shale, 263, 266; using, 317

Sediments [SEHD-uh-muhnts]: pieces of broken rock and other material deposited in layers on sea or land, 256; coal forming, 303, 305, 332; oil forming, 307, 308, 309, 332; and rock cycle, 269. *See also* Sedimentary rock

Seeds, food stored in, 285; growth and ripening of, 294; and living resources, 323; made from ovules and pollen, 291, 292; plants from, 286–291

Shale [shayl]: a soft sedimentary rock formed from clay; fossils found in, 263; oil, 316; porousness of, 310; slate formed from, 266

Skeleton [SKEHL-uh-tuhn]: a framework for the body; bones of, 80–88, 104; of insects, 6, 7, 36; in sediments, 257, 258

Skull [skuhl]: the bone that gives the head its shape, 80

Slate [slayt]: a hard, smooth, metamorphic rock formed from shale, 266

Smelting [SMEHLT-ihng]: heating metal ore to a very high temperature to get rid of wastes, 320

Social [SOH-shuhl]: insects, 25–31, 36

Soil, conserving, 329; materials for food from, 277; poison in, 33, 36; as a resource, 300; wearing out, 325

Solar system [SOH-luhr SIHS-tuhm]: the system formed by the sun, the planets, their moons, and the asteroids, 182–189, 202, 238; asteroids in, 218–219; Earth, 190–198, 208–209; Earth's moon, 209; Jupiter, 218–223; Mars, 198, 200, 201, 214–219; Mercury, 182, 210–211; Neptune, 229–230; Pluto, 230–231; Saturn, 223–226; Uranus, 227; Venus, 198, 212–213. *See also* Sun

Solid [SAHL-ihd]: matter in a state that keeps its shape, and heat energy, 130–

131; matter as, 132–133, 136; molecules of, 120, 121, 124

Space shuttle, 236–237

Stamen [STAY-muhn]: the pollen-making part of a flower, 287, 289, 290, 294

Stars, 181, 199

Stems, kinds of, 283, 284; tubes in, 282–283, 294

Storms, on Jupiter, 221

Sugar, and plants, 278, 279, 285, 294

Sun, and comets, 228; gravitation of, 184–186, 202; and solar system, 182–185. *See also* Solar system

Sunlight, and green plants, 275–278, 294; reflected by planets, 181; and rotation of Earth, 191–192; and seasons, 193–198; stored in coal, 304; stored in oil, 315; warming the earth, 160–161. *See also* Energy

Support, in plants, 283, 285, 294; skeleton as, 79–82, 104

System [SIHS-tuhm]: any group whose members act on each other, 183, 184

Telescopes [TEHL-uh-skohps]: devices for studying objects in space, 207, 224, 229, 231, 238

Temperature, and air's mass, 157–158; and air pressure, 174; of atmosphere, 141, 164–167; and conserving fuels, 328; below the earth's surface, 246; Earth's tilt and, 193–198; of land and water, 160–163; on Mars, 216; on Mercury, 211; and movement of air, 160, 166–167, 168–171, 174; on Neptune, 229; on Pluto, 230; on Uranus, 227; on Venus, 213

Tendons [TEHN-duhnz]: cords that attach muscles to bones, 99, 100, 104

Thorax [THOHR-aks]: a body part of insects, 5

Tilt [tihlt]: 193–198, 202, 216

Time, and coal formation, 302, 303, 332; and crystal size, 253–255, 270; and life cycles, 322–323, 332; for planet's revolution, 188–189; and rock cycle, 268–269, 270

Tubes, in people, 102, 103; in plants, 282–283, 285, 294

Uranus [YUR-uh-nuhs]: the seventh planet in the solar system, 182, 227, 229, 238

Veins [vaynz]: tubes in plants that carry food and water, 285; ore deposits in, 318, 319

Venus [VEE-nuhs]: the second planet from the sun in the solar system, 182, 198, 201, 212–213, 238

Volcanoes [vahl-KAY-nohz]: openings in a planet's surface through which liquid rock and gases escape, on Earth, 247; igneous rocks from, 253; on Jupiter, 223; on Mars, 215; and metamorphic rock formation, 267; on Venus, 213, 238

Waste, of resources, 325, 332

Water, changing temperature of, 160–163; from liquid to gas state, 125–127; made of hydrogen and oxygen, 119; and photosynthesis, 279; and plant roots, 279–281, 294; in plant tubes, 282–283, 285; poison in, 34, 36; pollution of, 325; as a resource, 300; from solid to liquid state, 122, 123; sun's heat and, 160–162, 174; used by plants to make food, 278

Water vapor [WAW-tuhr VAY-puhr]: water in the atmosphere in the form of a gas, 144, 148, 156–157; used to study air pressure, 151

Wedge [wehj]: a kind of machine, 58–59, 74

Wheel and axle, a kind of machine, 64, 74; making work easier with, 65–66; of pulley, 60

Wind, movement of air resulting from unequal heating, 168–171; pollen spread by, 291

Wings, of insects, 7

CREDITS

Illustrations Roberta Aggarwal: 193 / Laurel Aiello: 135 / Steven Alexander from Gwen Goldstein: 54 bottom, 157, 278 top, 279 bottom, 283 top, 287 left, 292 / ANCO Boston: 21 lower right, 49, 84 bottom, 107, 120 bottom, 130 bottom, 133, 144, 156 bottom, 164, 185 bottom, 187 bottom, 232, 234, 278 bottom / Robert Anderson: 139, 162, 168, 169, 203, 333 / Davis Meltzer: 211, 218 / Irene Roman from Gwen Goldstein: 146, 149, 152 right, 166, 170 / Laurel Smith: 290 bottom / James Teason: 5, 27 left, 88, 89, 90, 91, 92, 94, 96, 100, 101, 102, 122, 125 bottom, 153 bottom, 154 bottom, 171, 183, 185 top, 187 top, 194 bottom, 196, 197, 227, 228 top, 229, 230, 247 top, 248 bottom, 257 left, 260, 268, 280 bottom, 284, 285, 302, 303 top, 305, 307, 310, 312, 320 bottom / William Tenney: 139, 199 / George Ulrich: 39, 76, 77, 106, 138, 177, 204, 205, 240, 241, 273, 296, 297, 335

Photography Alcan Aluminum Corporation: 327 left and lower right / Aluminum Association: 327 top / American Petroleum Institute: 316 / Erik Anderson: 295 / Philip Jon Bailey: 2, 36, 74, 78, 104, 136 / Duane Bradford: 291 top / Elaine Brock: 113 middle right / Richard Weymouth Brooks, Photo Researchers: 258 top / J. D. Bulger, Photo Researchers: 173 lower right / William Byrne: 7 lower left, 21 top / Carlye Calvin: 44 upper left, right, 46 lower left, 113 lower right, 125 top, 172 lower left, 173 upper left, 257 upper right, 320 top / A. James Casner III: 54 top, 55, 65, 73, 98, 110, 115 left, 116 middle, 117, 145, 147, 148, 154 top, 156 top, 251, 254, 259, 276, 282 lower left / Porterfield Chickering, Photo Researchers: 173 upper right, 321 upper right / Colour Library International: 242 / John Colwell from Grant Heilman: 155 upper middle / Dr. E. R. Degginger: 4 lower left, 10 upper left, 11 lower right, 12, 15, 19 middle top, 22 top, 46 upper left, 61 lower right, 113, 172 upper left, 263 left, 266 top middle, top right, 317 lower left / Dennis Di Cicco: 180 / Margaret Durrance, Photo Researchers: 152 left / William E. Ferguson, Nature Photography: 4 upper left, upper right, middle right, 6 middle right, lower left, 7 upper left, middle left, middle right, 10 lower middle right, 11 upper left, lower left, middle right, 18, 21 lower left, 23 upper right, 24 upper right, lower left, lower middle, lower right, 172 lower right, 257 lower right, 261 upper right, 263 lower right, 266 top left, 267, 331 / Focus on Sports: 113 bottom right / John E. Fogle: 61 lower left, 294 / Jeffrey Jay Foxx, Woodfin Camp and Associates: 40 / Howard J. Gordon, Reflections: 44 lower left / Martin Grossmann: 228 / Ned Haines, Photo Researchers: 172 upper right / Walter E. Harvey, NAS, Photo Researchers: 290 top / Grant Heilman: 4 lower right, 29 bottom, 257 middle right, 265 right, 269, 300, 321 upper left, 323, 324, 330 / W. H. Hodge, Peter Arnold, Inc.: 283 lower right, 291 lower right / Tom Hughes, Photo